Josephine Preston Peabody, William Douw Lighthall

Canadian Poems and Lays

Selections of Native Verse, Reflecting the Seasons, Legends, and Life of the

Dominion

Josephine Preston Peabody, William Douw Lighthall

Canadian Poems and Lays
Selections of Native Verse, Reflecting the Seasons, Legends, and Life of the Dominion

ISBN/EAN: 9783337155056

Printed in Europe, USA, Canada, Australia, Japan

Cover: Foto ©ninafisch / pixelio.de

More available books at **www.hansebooks.com**

The Canterbury Poets.
Edited by William Sharp.

CANADIAN POEMS AND LAYS.

.·. FOR FULL LIST OF THE VOLUMES IN THIS SERIES,
SEE CATALOGUE AT END OF BOOK.

CANADIAN POEMS AND LAYS: SELECTIONS OF NATIVE VERSE, REFLECTING THE SEASONS, LEGENDS, AND LIFE OF THE DOMINION.

ARRANGED AND EDITED BY
WILLIAM DOUW LIGHTHALL, M.A.,
OF MONTREAL.

LONDON:
WALTER SCOTT, LIMITED,
24 WARWICK LANE.

Dedication.

To history's vastest Brotherhood,—
   Which seas that girdle earth but bind:
To every man of British blood:—
   To all of the Imperial mind;
Or who, of any noble race, have by the Empire stood.

What matter races! vain the pride
   Who first this brotherhood began;
Than Pict or Gael we grow more wide,
   Our final brotherhood is Man:
Unto all union we will hold, so Man yet onward stride.

And you, great kinsmen scarcely lost,
   Alliance with you still increase:—
With you the kindliest, first, and most
   Union for justice, trade, and peace!
States are the robes that suit the climes: we move,
   one spirit host.

This March night, gleams the elm-lined street
   With pools beneath a rising moon;
In the West's brow bright Venus sweet
   Holds Nature in a lovelorn swoon;
Go, songs, glint what these lands shall be in wondrous
   Day complete.

CONTENTS.

	PAGE
ENTRY OF THE MINSTRELS. *"The Masque of Minstrels"*	xv
ARTHUR J. LOCKHART.	
INTRODUCTION	xvii

I.—THE IMPERIAL SPIRIT.

HASTINGS . . *"Merlin, and Other Poems"*		3
JOHN READE.		
CANADA TO ENGLAND		6
ANONYMOUS.		
EMPIRE FIRST		8
JOHN TALON-LESPÉRANCE—"LACLÈDE."		
THE CANADIANS ON THE NILE . . *"Poems"*		9
WILLIAM WYE SMITH.		

II.—THE NEW NATIONALITY.

DOMINION DAY	13
"FIDELIS."	
CANADA . . . *"In Divers Tones"*	16
CHARLES G. D. ROBERTS.	

CONTENTS.

	PAGE
THE CONFUSED DAWN *"Thoughts, Moods, and Ideals"*	18
WILLIAM DOUW LIGHTHALL.	
FROM "'85"	19
BARRY STRATTON.	
CANADA NOT LAST *"Thoughts, Moods, and Ideals"*	19
WILLIAM DOUW LIGHTHALL.	
COLLECT FOR DOMINION DAY *"In Divers Tones"*	21
CHARLES G. D. ROBERTS.	

III.—THE INDIAN.

A BLOOD-RED RING HUNG ROUND THE MOON	25
JOHN E. LOGAN—"BARRY DANE."	
THE DEPARTING OF CLOTE SCARP *"In Divers Tones"*	26
CHARLES G. D. ROBERTS.	
FROM "TECUMSEH"—ACT I., SCENE 2	28
CHARLES MAIR.	
THE ARCTIC INDIAN'S FAITH *"Poems"*	30
THOMAS D'ARCY M'GEE.	
THE CAUGHNAWAGA BEADWORK-SELLER	31
WILLIAM DOUW LIGHTHALL.	
FROM "WAHONOMIN" *"Poems"*	32
FREDERICK GEORGE SCOTT.	
CAUGHNAWAGA SONG	34
Tr. JOHN WANIENTE JOCKS.	

IV.—THE VOYAGEUR AND HABITANT.

THE OLD RÉGIME *"Song of Welcome"*	39
MRS. J. F. W. HARRISON—"SERANUS."	
MALBROUCK *Old Chanson*	42
Tr. WILLIAM M'LENNAN.	

CONTENTS.

	PAGE
À LA CLAIRE FONTAINE . . . *Old Chanson*	44
Tr. WILLIAM DOUW LIGHTHALL.	
EN ROULANT MA BOULÉ . . . *Old Chanson*	46
Tr. WILLIAM M'LENNAN.	
ENTRE PARIS ET SAINT-DENIS . . *Old Chanson*	48
Tr. WILLIAM M'LENNAN.	
MARIANSON . . . . . *Old Chanson*	50
Tr. WILLIAM M'LENNAN.	
THE RE-SETTLEMENT OF ACADIA	54
ARTHUR WENTWORTH EATON.	
AT THE CEDARS	58
DUNCAN CAMPBELL SCOTT.	
ROSE LATULIPPE . *A French Canadian Legend*	61
MRS. J. F. W. HARRISON—"SERANUS."	
ADIEU TO FRANCE . . . "*De Roberval*"	70
JOHN HUNTER-DUVAR.	

V.—SETTLEMENT LIFE.

SONG OF THE AXE . . "*Old Spookses' Pass*"	75
ISABELLA VALANCEY CRAWFORD.	
FIRE IN THE WOODS; OR, THE OLD SETTLER'S STORY	76
ALEXANDER M'LACHLAN.	
BURNT LANDS	81
CHARLES G. D. ROBERTS.	
FROM "MALCOLM'S KATIE" "*Old Spookses' Pass*"	84
ISABELLA VALANCEY CRAWFORD.	
THE SECOND CONCESSION OF DEER . "*Poems*"	87
WILLIAM WYE SMITH.	
A CANADIAN FOLK-SONG "*Snowflakes and Sunbeams*"	89
WILLIAM WILFRED CAMPBELL.	
"THE INJUN" . . *Incident of Minnesota Massacre*	90
JOHN E. LOGAN—"BARRY DANE."	

CONTENTS.

VI.—SPORTS AND FREE LIFE.

	PAGE
THE WRAITH OF THE RED SWAN	99
BLISS CARMAN.	
BIRCH AND PADDLE . . ."*In Divers Tones*"	105
CHARLES G. D. ROBERTS.	
THE NOR'-WEST COURIER	108
JOHN E. LOGAN—"BARRY DANE."	
THE HALL OF SHADOWS . "*Poems and Songs*"	110
ALEXANDER M'LACHLAN.	
CANADIAN HUNTER'S SONG	114
MRS. SUSANNA (STRICKLAND) MOODIE.	
THE FISHERMAN'S LIGHT . *A Song of the Backwoods*	115
MRS. SUSANNA (STRICKLAND) MOODIE.	
THE KINGFISHER	116
CHARLES LEE BARNES.	
THE CANOE . . . "*Old Spookses' Pass*"	117
ISABELLA VALANCEY CRAWFORD.	
CANOE SONG . . . "*Old Spookses' Pass*"	120
ISABELLA VALANCEY CRAWFORD.	
THE WALKER OF THE SNOW	121
CHARLES DAWSON SHANLY.	
THE RAPID . . . . (*St. Lawrence*)	124
CHARLES SANGSTER.	
THE WINTER SPIRIT . . (*Origin of the Ice Palace*)	125
HELEN FAIRBAIRN.	
SNOWSHOEING SONG	127
ARTHUR WEIR.	
SKATING .	129
JOHN LOWRY STUART.	
THE WINTER CARNIVAL	131
JOHN READE.	
THE SPIRIT OF THE CARNIVAL	134
"FLEURANGE."	

CONTENTS.

VII.—THE SPIRIT OF CANADIAN HISTORY.

		PAGE
JACQUES CARTIER . . . . "*Poems*"		143
HON. THOMAS D'ARCY M'GEE.		
THE CAPTURED FLAG . . . "*Fleurs de Lys*"		146
ARTHUR WEIR.		
HOW CANADA WAS SAVED		149
GEORGE MURRAY.		
MADELEINE DE VERCHÈRES		155
JOHN READE.		
THE BATTLE OF LA PRAIRIE . . *A Ballad*		161
WILLIAM DOUW LIGHTHALL.		
THE BATTLE OF GRAND PRÉ		163
M. J. KATZMANN LAWSON.		
SPINA CHRISTI . . . . "*Canadian Idylls*"		167
WILLIAM KIRBY.		
THE LOYALISTS		181
SARAH ANNE CURZON.		
BROCK		182
CHARLES SANGSTER.		
TECUMSEH'S DEATH . . . "*Tecumseh*"		184
MAJOR RICHARDSON.		
A BALLAD FOR BRAVE WOMEN		185
CHARLES MAIR.		
THE VETERAN		190
J. A. FRASER.		
IN HOSPITAL		191
ANNIE ROTHWELL.		
IN MEMORIAM . . . "*The Soul's Quest*"		196
FREDERICK GEORGE SCOTT.		

VIII.—PLACES.

THE TANTRAMAR REVISITED . "*In Divers Tones*"		201
ANONYMOUS.		

CONTENTS.

	PAGE
LOW TIDE ON GRAND PRÉ . . .	204
BLISS CARMAN.	
THE INDIAN NAMES OF ACADIA . .	207
Attributed to DE MILLE.	
ON LEAVING THE COAST OF NOVA SCOTIA *"Poems"*	208
GEORGE FREDERICK CAMERON.	
THE FAIRIES IN PRINCE EDWARD ISLAND . .	209
JOHN HUNTER-DUVAR.	
THE VALE OF THE GASPEREAU . .	211
ARTHUR JOHN LOCKHART.	
THE ISLE OF DEMONS . . *"Marguerite"*	212
GEORGE MARTIN.	
SAGUENAY	218
J. D. EDGAR.	
QUEBEC . . *"St. Lawrence and Saguenay"*	219
CHARLES SANGSTER.	
MONTREAL	220
WILLIAM M'LENNAN.	
THE ST. LAWRENCE	221
K. L. JONES.	
NIGHT IN THE THOUSAND ISLES . *"St. Lawrence and Saguenay"*	222
CHARLES SANGSTER.	
OTTAWA	224
DUNCAN CAMPBELL SCOTT.	
AT THE FERRY	224
E. PAULINE JOHNSON.	
NIAGARA	226
WILLIAM KIRBY.	
THE HEART OF THE LAKES	228
WILLIAM WILFRED CAMPBELL.	
MANITOU . . . . *"Lake Lyrics"*	229
WILLIAM WILFRED CAMPBELL.	

CONTENTS.

		PAGE
THE LAST BISON		231
CHARLES MAIR.		
A PRAIRIE YEAR	"*Eos: A Prairie Dream*"	237
NICHOLAS FLOOD DAVIS.		
THE LEGEND OF THUNDER	"*Western Life*"	239
H. R. A. POCOCK.		

IX.—SEASONS.

HEAT	"*In the Millet*"	251
ARCHIBALD LAMPMAN.		
THE FIR WOODS		253
CHARLES G. D. ROBERTS.		
CLOUDS	"*In the Millet*"	253
ARCHIBALD LAMPMAN.		
FROGS		254
CHARLES G. D. ROBERTS.		
TWILIGHT	"*Jephthah's Daughter*"	255
CHARLES HEAVYSEGE.		
A CANADIAN SUMMER EVENING	"*Poems*"	255
MRS. LEPROHON.		
EVENING ON THE MARSHES		256
BARRY STRATON.		
MIDSUMMER NIGHT	"*In the Millet*"	257
ARCHIBALD LAMPMAN.		
OCTOBER	"*Poems and Songs*"	258
ALEXANDER M'LACHLAN.		
FIRST SNOW		260
JOHN TALON-LESPÉRANCE—"LACLÈDE."		
INDIAN SUMMER		261
WILLIAM WILFRED CAMPBELL.		

CONTENTS.

	PAGE
AN INDIAN SUMMER CAROL . . . . . "FIDELIS."	262
A MID-WINTER NIGHT'S DREAM . *"Snowflakes and Sunbeams"* . . . . . . WILLIAM WILFRED CAMPBELL.	264
WINTER NIGHT . . *"Jephthah's Daughter"* CHARLES HEAVYSEGE.	265
ICICLE DROPS . . . . *From "Canada"* ARTHUR JOHN LOCKHART.	265
THE SILVER FROST . . . . . BARRY STRATON.	266
THE JEWELLED TREES. . . . . GEORGE MARTIN.	268
IN LYRIC SEASON . . . . . . BLISS CARMAN.	270
THE FROGS . . . . *"In the Millet"* ARCHIBALD LAMPMAN.	271
THE CANADIAN SONG-SPARROW . . . . J. D. EDGAR.	273
IN JUNE. . . . . E. W. THOMSON.	274

ENTRY OF THE MINSTRELS.

From "THE MASQUE OF MINSTRELS."

Arthur J. Lockhart.

Then came a company of wandering minstrels, without singing robes and garlands, up to the gate of the castle, which was opened readily enough to receive them. They were now only in the court-yard; but they went on—their harps in their hands—strengthened by the countenances of one another, and unabashed by the mighty band who had gone in before them. They were late in coming, and the choir of singers was already full; but of this they thought no ill, and when questioned of their act they answered with a proud humility. They were near the door of the high hall, and in answer to their summons it was thrown open, so that a herald stood before them.

HERALD.

And who be ye?

FIRST MINSTREL.

We be also of the Minstrelsy; we be Apprentices of the Muses; Secretaries of Love; Slaves of Beauty; Apostles of Desire; Disciples of Truth; Children of Nature; Followers of Aspiration; Servants of Song. We be uncrowned kings and queens in the realms of Music, coming to claim and win our sceptres. Crowns have been won and worn by others. Admit us.

HERALD.

Nay; ye claim too largely. Whose sons be ye, and whose daughters?

SECOND MINSTREL.

We be sons and daughters of fathers who were never cowards, and of mothers who were never ashamed; who loved valour and virtue even as their children love music.

INTRODUCTION.

THE poets whose songs fill this book are voices cheerful with the consciousness of young might, public wealth, and heroism. Through them, taken all together, you may catch something of great Niagara falling, of brown rivers rushing with foam, of the crack of the rifle in the haunts of the moose and caribou, the lament of vanishing races singing their death-song as they are swept on to the cataract of oblivion, the rural sounds of Arcadias just rescued from surrounding wildernesses by the axe, shrill war-whoops of Iroquois battle, proud traditions of contests with the French and the Americans, stern and sorrowful cries of valour rising to curb rebellion. The tone of them is *courage;*—for to hunt, to fight, to hew out a farm, one must be a man! Through their new hopes, doubts, exultations, questionings, the virility of fighting races is the undertone. Canadians are, for the most part, the descendants of armies, officers and men, and every generation of them has stood up to battle.

The delight of a Clear Atmosphere runs through it too, and the rejoicings of the Winter Carnival; with the glint of that heavenly Palace of illumined pearl, which is the February pilgrimage of North America.

b

INTRODUCTION.

Canada, Eldest Daughter of the Empire, is the Empire's completest type! She is the full-grown of the family,—the one first come of age and gone out into life as a nation; and she has in her young hands the solution of all those questions which must so interest every true Briton, proud and careful of the acquisitions of British discovery and conquest. She is Imperial in herself, we sons of her think, as the number, the extent, and the lavish natural wealth of her Provinces, each not less than some empire of Europe, rises in our minds; as we picture her coasts and gulfs and kingdoms and islands, on the Atlantic on one side, and the Pacific on the other; her four-thousand-mile panorama of noble rivers, wild forests, ocean-like prairies; her towering snow-capped Rockies waking to the tints of sunrise in the West; in the East her hoary Laurentians, oldest of hills. She has by far the richest extent of fisheries, forests, wheat lands, and fur regions in the world; some of the greatest public works; some of the loftiest mountain-ranges, the vastest rivers, the healthiest and most beautifully varied seasons. She has the best ten-elevenths of Niagara Falls, and the best half of the Inland Seas. She stands fifth among the nations in the tonnage of her commercial marine. Her population is about five million souls. Her Valley of the Saskatchewan alone, it has been scientifically computed, will support eight hundred millions. In losing the United States, Britain lost the *smaller* half of her American possessions:—the Colony of the Maple Leaf is about as large as Europe.

But what would material resources be without a corresponding greatness in man? Canada is also Imperial in her traditions. Her French race are still conscious that they are the remnants of a power which once ruled North America from Hudson's Bay to the Gulf of Mexico. Existing English Canada is the result of simply the noblest epic migration the world has ever seen:—more loftily epic than the retirement of Pius Æneas from Ilion, —the withdrawal, namely, out of the rebel Colonies, of the thirty-five thousand United Empire Loyalists after the War of the Revolution. " Why did you come here ? " was asked of one of the first settlers of St. John, New Brunswick, a man whose life was without a stain;— " Why did you come here, when you and your associates were almost certain to endure the sufferings and absolute want of shelter and food which you have narrated?" "*Why did we come here?*" replied he, with emotion which brought tears :—" *For our loyalty.*"

Canada has, of historic right, a voice also in the Empire of to-day, and busies herself not a little in studying its problems. For example, the question whether that Empire will last is being asked. Her history has a reply to that :—IT WILL, IF IT SETS CLEARLY BEFORE IT A DEFINITE IDEAL THAT MEN WILL SUFFER AND DIE FOR ; and such an Ideal—worthy of long and patient endeavour—may be found in broad-minded advance towards the voluntary Federation of Mankind. She has a special history, too, which even under the overshadowing greatness of that of the Empire—in which she also owns her part—is one of interest. First explored in 1535, by Jacques-Cartier, of St. Malo, by command of Francis I., and its settlement established in 1608 through the foundation of Quebec by the devoted and energetic Maker of French Canada, Samuel de Champlain, its story down to the Conquest in 1759-63 is full of romance, —Jesuit missionaries, explorers, chevaliers, painted Indian war-parties, the rich fur trade, and finally the great struggle under Montcalm, closing with his expiry and Wolfe's at the hour of the fall of Quebec, passing like a panorama. Then came the entry of the Loyalists, and from that to the present there has been a steady unfolding to power and culture, broken only by the brave war of 1812, and a French, and two half-breed, rebellions. She is, to-day, next to the United States, the strongest factor in American affairs.

The Literature of this daughter-nation in the West, as distilled by its poets, ought to be interesting to Englishmen. That other Colonial poetic literature presented in the Australian volume, has shown that there can be a signal attractiveness in such a picture of a fresh world. On the part of Canada the semi-tropical Australian surroundings are matched in beauty by a Northern atmosphere of objects which make vivid contrasts with them; her native races were the noblest of savage tribes; while the Imperial and National feelings, developing in two such different hemispheres, are instructive in their divergences and similarities. The romantic life of each Colony also has a special flavour, —Australian rhyme is a poetry of the *horse;* Canadian, of the *canoe.*

Now, who are those who are drinking these inspirations and breathing them into song? In communing with them, we shall try to transport you to the Canadian clime itself. You shall come out with us as a guest of its skies and air, paddling over bright lakes and down savage rivers; singing French *chansons* to the swing of our paddles, till we come into the settlements; and shall be swept along on great rafts of timber by the majestic St. Lawrence, to moor at historic cities whose streets and harbours are thronged with the commerce of all Europe and the world. You shall hear there the chants of a new nationality, weaving in with songs of the Empire, of its heroes, of its Queen.

A word first about the *personnel* of our conductors. The foremost name in Canadian song at the present day is that of Charles George Douglas Roberts, poet, canoeist, and Professor of Literature, who has struck the supreme note of Canadian nationality in his "Canada" and "Ode for the Canadian Confederacy." His claim to supremacy lies, for the rest, chiefly in the quality of the two volumes, "Orion and other Poems," which he published in 1880 at the age of twenty-one, and "In Divers Tones," which appeared in 1887. The style and taste of Roberts at its best are characterised by two different elements—a striking predilection for the pictorial ideals and nature-poetry of classical Greece; and a noble passion, whose fire and music resemble and approach Tennyson's. "Orion," "Actæon," "Off Pelorus," and "The Pipes of Pan" are purely Greek, drawn direct from "ancient founts of inspiration." On the other hand, his "O Child of Nations, giant-limbed!" which stirs every true Canadian like a trumpet, is, though of different subject and metre, of the stamp and calibre of "Locksley Hall."

Roberts loves his country fervently, as is apparent in all his Canadian themes. His heart dwells with fondness on the scenes of his Maritime Provinces, "the long dikes of Tantramar," and the ebb-tide sighing out, "reluctant for the reed-beds;" and he was one of the first to sing Confederation. His sympathy is also Britain's—

> " Let a great wrong cry to heaven,
> Let a giant necessity come;
> And now as of old she can strike,
> She will strike, and strike home!"

In point of time, however, the first important national poet was not Roberts, but nature-loving Charles Sangster, a born son of the Muses, and who was long the people's favourite. Sangster is a kind of Wordsworth, with rather more fire, and of course a great deal less metaphysical and technical skill. He has the unevenness and frequent flatness of Wordsworth, but is as close a personal friend of the mountains, lakes, and woods.

"I have laid my cheek to Nature's, put my puny hands in hers."

Glowingly he takes us, in "St. Lawrence and the Saguenay," down the grandeurs of that unrivalled tour—the great River, its rapids, cities, mountains, and "Isles of the Blest."

Sangster's nervous system was broken down by the grind of newspaper toil and civil service tread-milling, and he has not written or published for twenty years; yet, though poetry has till lately been given a particularly small share of attention in Canada, his "Brock," his lines on Quebec, and many striking passages from his poems, are treasured in the popular memory.

But the most striking volume next to those of Roberts —indeed more boldly new than his—is that of the late brilliant Isabella Valancey Crawford. This wonderful girl, living in the "Empire" Province of Ontario, early saw the possibilities of the new field around her, and had she lived longer might have made a really matchless name. It was only in 1884 that her modest blue card-covered volume of two hundred and twenty-four pages came out. The sad story of unrecognised genius and death was re-enacted. "Old Spookses' Pass; Malcolm's Katie, and other Poems," as it was doubly entitled (the names at least were against it!), almost dropped from the press. Scarcely anybody noticed it in Canada. It made no stir, and in little more than two years the authoress died. She was a high-spirited, passionate girl, and there is very little doubt that the neglect her book received was the cause of her death. Afterwards, as usual, a good many people began to find they had overlooked work of merit. Miss Crawford's verse was, in fact, seen to be phenomenal. Setting aside her dialect

INTRODUCTION. xxiii

poems, like "Old Spookses' Pass" (which, though the dialect is a trifle artificial, resulted in hitting off some good pictures of imaginary rustic characters), the style peculiarly her own has seldom been equalled for strength, colour, and originality—

> "Low the sun beat on the land,
>   Purple slope and olive wood;
> With the wine-cup in his hand,
>   Vast the Helot herdsman stood."
>
> . . . . .
>
> "Day was at her high unrest;
>   Fevered with the wine of light,
> Loosing all her golden vest,
>   Reeled she towards the coming Night."

Miss Crawford's poetry is packed with fine stuff. It is worth a share of attention from the whole Anglo-Saxon world. The splendour of Canadian colour, the wonderful blue skies of that clear climate, the Heaven's-forests of its autumn, the matchless American sunsets and sunrises, imbued her like Roberts. A poetess of such original nature could not but strike boldly into Canadian subjects. "Malcolm's Katie; a Love Story," is an idyl of a true man who goes forth and cuts him a home with his axe, and of a maiden who remains true to him, until he returns for their union. Few finer bits were ever written by any one or anywhere than the passage which we give, from "Shanties grew," down to its glorious climax in the song, "O Love will build his lily walls." It seems to us that this is the most effective known use of a lyric introduced into a long poem. Her works, including a good deal never yet published, were about to be brought before the English public in a new volume. A letter of hers concerning the unpublished material, stated that it contained some of her best work.

The poets best known and most favourite next to Roberts and Sangster are—besides Isabella Crawford—

M'Lachlan, Kirby, and tender-hearted John Reade. Reade is one the charms of whose style are sweetness and culture. He is best known by his "Merlin, and Other Poems" (1870), composed of short lyrics, led off by "The Prophecy of Merlin," which is a Tennysonian Idyll of the King, foreshadowing the greatness of the British Empire. His style turns everything it touches into grace, but it appeals to the inner circle rather than the folk, and seems to shrink away from touching organ-keys. For examples of this grace of his, I should like to quote his "The Inexpressible," or "Good Night," but cannot do so here.

The claim of first place is awarded by the feelings of no small number to Alexander M'Lachlan, the human-hearted, vigorous Scottish Radical, whose stanzas have such a singing rhythm and direct sympathy. They were a few years ago made a special feature of the great comic paper *Grip*, the *Punch* of Canada, and his popularity is shown by the presentation by his admirers a short time since of a homestead farm, upon which he now lives. His "Idylls of the Dominion," from which the poems quoted in this book are principally drawn, are so characteristic both of himself and of pioneerdom, that he is called "The Burns of Canada."

William Kirby deserves a high position for his beautiful "Canadian Idylls" (based on history, while M'Lachlan's are upon life), from which "Spina Christi" is drawn. There are also some able descriptions in his long-known "U. E." (Loyalist) poem, from which is taken his passage on Niagara. Steeped in the romance of Canadian history, he wrote many years ago a magnificent novel founded upon the Quebec legend of the Chien d'Or, which has remained the most popular of Canadian stories. Kirby's strong point is his graphic descriptions.

One name I have not yet pronounced, though every

Canadian no doubt has looked for it. A sombre shadow towers in the background of the group,—a man apart from the rest,—Charles Heavysege, author of the drama "Saul." When "Saul" came out in 1857, and a copy fell into the hands of Nathaniel Hawthorne, Heavysege became famous. He was pronounced the greatest dramatist since Shakespeare. The *North British Review* for August 1858 spoke of the book as follows:—

"Of 'Saul, a Drama, in three parts,' published anonymously at Montreal, we have before us perhaps the only copy which has crossed the Atlantic. At all events we have heard of no other, as it is probable we should have done, through some public or private notice, seeing that the work is indubitably one of the most remarkable English poems ever written out of Great Britain."

The *North British* reviewer was later by no means alone in its praise, and it became the fashion among tourists to Montreal to buy a copy of "Saul."

Heavysege had a very strange and original cast of mind. The following brief poem may be read as being characteristic of him :—

"Open, my heart, thy ruddy valves;
  It is thy master calls;
Let me go down, and curious trace
  Thy labyrinthine halls.
Open, O heart, and let me view
  The secrets of thy den;
Myself unto myself now show
  With introspective ken.
Expose thyself, thou covered nest
  Of passions, and be seen;
Stir up thy brood, that in unrest
  Are ever piping keen.
Ah! what a motley multitude,
  Magnanimous and mean!"

He was originally a drama-composing carpenter, then a journalist in Montreal, and wore out his soul at the drudgery of the latter occupation and in poverty. To get out the third edition of "Saul" he was forced to borrow the money, which he was never able to repay. In person he was a small, very reticent man, who walked along the streets altogether locked up in himself, so that a literary acquaintance of his says Heavysege's appearance always reminded him of "The Yellow Dwarf,"—

> "He walked our streets, and no one knew
> That something of celestial hue
> Had passed along; a toil-worn man
> Was seen,—no more; the fire that ran
> Electric through his veins, and wrought
> Sublimity of soul and thought,
> And kindled into song, no eye
> Beheld."

He died in 1869. A man apart he has remained. His work is in no sense distinctively Canadian. Canadians do not read him; but they claim him as perhaps their greatest, most original writer, if they could weigh him aright and appreciate him.

Sympathy with the prairie and the Indian has produced the best verse of Charles Mair, who has dramatised the story of the immortal British ally Tecumseh, and lately from his North-West home gives us "The Last Bison"; and who has lived a life almost as Indian and North-West as his poems. "The Last Bison," he says, was suggested to him by what happened before his own eyes near the elbow of the North Saskatchewan some eight years ago. "Not a buffalo," so far as he knows, "has been seen on that river since. There are some animals in private collections; a small band perhaps exists in the fastnesses of Montana, and a few wood buffaloes still roam the Mackenzie River region; but the wild bison of the plains may now be looked upon as extinct." We may add, that it was lately reported by an Indian that he had tracked a herd of seven in the northerly region of the Peace River. He shot four bulls and a calf out of the seven! The North-West has also given happy inspirations to "Barry Dane" as a bird of passage.

John Hunter-Duvar, the author of "De Roberval" and Squire of "Hernewood," in Prince Edward Island, described in "The Emigration of the Fairies," derives his verse largely from the life and legends of the surrounding regions, shaped by his good library.

George Martin, of Montreal, has digged in the goldmine of old French legend, with the result of "Marguerite; or, The Isle of Demons," a weird and sad story of De Roberval's desertion of his niece in one of the early expeditions.

Arthur Wentworth Eaton and George Murray have explored the same mine with signal success—the latter, who is very well known as a *litterateur*, producing the fine ballad, "How Canada was Saved." The same story has been well put in Martin's "Heroes of Ville-Marie."

Bliss Carman has earned special honour for the originality and finish of his lyrics. Arthur John Lockhart, in his "Masque of Minstrels,"—particularly in "Gaspereau,"—sings as a bird of exile warbling towards home, for he lives just over the frontier. William Wilfred Campbell is the poet of the Great Lakes, which he has studied with a perfect love, resulting in those beautiful "Lake Lyrics" of his, which the reader will stop to admire. A bit of work of particular attractiveness has been done by William M'Lennan in his well-known translations of the old French *chansons*. Archibald Lampman has written perfectly exquisite pre-Raphaelite descriptions with the finish and sparkle of jewellers' work.

I should have liked to quote more fully than has been

possible from the "Lyrics on Freedom, Love, and Death" of the late George Frederick Cameron; but his fire and generosity of spirit belong rather to the world than to Canadian inspiration, and we are therefore confined here to a few lesser pieces of his. He died early, like so many other sons of genius.

Among names of special grace or promise are to be added those of "Laclède," John Talon-Lespérance, the well-known *littérateur*, and Fellow of the Royal Society of Canada; Barry Straton, Duncan Campbell Scott, Frederick George Scott, John Henry Brown, Dr. Æneas M'Donald Dawson, F.R.S.C.; Arthur Weir (the author of "Fleurs de Lys"); Dr. Charles Edwin Jakeway; the late Honourables d'Arcy M'Gee and Joseph Howe; Ernest J. Chapman, E. W. Thomson, Carroll Ryan, William Wye Smith, Phillips Stewart, J. J. Proctor, J. A. Richey; the aged but bright G. W. Wicksteed, Q.C.; H. L. Spencer; Messrs. Shanly, Dunn, Haliburton, M'Donell, James M'Carroll, J. H. Bowes, K. L. Jones, S. J. Watson, T. G. Marquis, M'Alpine Taylor, the late Francis Rye, the late John Lowry Stuart, the late Charles Pelham Mulvaney, H. R. A. Pocock (author of spirited North-West pieces), Alexander Rae Garvie, and M'Pherson, the early Nova Scotia singer, whose "I Long for Spring, enchanting Spring," has a bell-like silveriness. Some of these I have been unable to get at. A bright and erratic name, which I am sorry I cannot represent, is that of the journalist, George T. Lanigan ("Allid"), — "the most brilliant journalist who ever lived," says Mr. George Murray. Lanigan wrote with equal felicity in French and English, and his humour was inexhaustible. I regret that space forbids me to add in the body of the book two good things by D. B. Kerr and Emily M'Manus. The latter's subject is the crescent province of the West:—

"MANITOBA.

" Softly the shadows of prairie-land wheat
Ripple and riot adown to her feet;
Murmurs all Nature with joyous acclaim,
Fragrance of summer and shimmer of flame:
Heedless she hears while the centuries slip :—
Chalice of poppy is laid on her lip.

" Hark! From the East comes a ravishing note,—
Sweeter was never in nightingale's throat,—
Silence of centuries thrills to the song,
Singing their silence awaited so long;
Low, yet it swells to the heaven's blue dome,
Child-lips have called the wild meadow-land 'Home!'"

. . . .

One peculiar feature of this literature, indeed, is its strength in lady singers. The number who have produced true poetry seems to indicate something special in the conditions of a new country. Verily one has not to read far in that noble, patriotic book, "Laura Secord," to acknowledge that Mrs. Sarah Anne Curzon writes with the power and spirit of masculinity. The best war-songs of the late half-breed rebellion were written by Annie Rothwell, of Kingston. "Fidelis" (Agnes Maule Machar), who is frequently given the credit of being the first of our poetesses, shows some of the same spirit, but excels in a graceful subjectivity which unfortunately is unfitted for representative quotation here; a remark which applies with still more hapless effect to the philosophic thought of Mary Morgan ("Gowan Lea"). Agnes Seymour Maclean, authoress of "The Coming of the Princess," is mistress of a style of singular richness; and some of the brightest writing, both prose and verse, is done by "Seranus," of Toronto (Mrs. S. Frances Harrison), who is working good service to our literature in a number of ways. Her "Old Régime" and "Rose Latulippe" express what has been called her "half-French heart," and breathe the air of the fertile, scarcely-wrought field of French Canadian life. Then there are "Fleurange," who wrote the best Carnival Poem, "The Italian Boy's Dream"; E. Pauline Johnson, daughter of Head-Chief Johnson, of the Mohawks of Brantford, who gives us poetry of a high stamp, and of great interest on account of her descent; "Espérance" (Alice Maud Ardagh); Mrs. Leprohon; Mary Barry Smith; Helen Fairbairn; M. J. Katzmann Lawson; the late Miss E. M. Nash; Pamelia Vining Yule, "Clare Everest"; Janet Carnochan; Mrs. Edgar Jarvis, "Jeanie Gray"; Isabel Macpherson; Louisa Murray, a well-known authoress, who, besides much fine prose, has written "Merlin's Cave," one of the best of Canadian undistinctive poems; and Ethelwyn Wetherald, authoress of many exquisite sonnets. Even from the beginning—fifty years ago, for there was no native poetry to speak of before that—we had Susanna Moodie, one of the famous Strickland sisters, authoress of "Roughing it in the Bush," who gave us the best verses we had during many years, and some of the most patriotic.

Many more writers than those above named, in all to a number which might be roughly placed at three hundred, have at various times produced really good verse.

A curious Indian song, representing a small but unique song-literature which has sprung up among the tribe at Caughnawaga Reservation, near Montreal, *since* barbaric times, "from the sheer necessity of singing when together," was translated specially for me by Mr. John Waniente Jocks, the son of a Six-nation chief of that Reservation.

A few general remarks are now in order. The present is by no means a perfect presentation of Canadian poetry from a purely literary point of view, on account of the limitation of treatment; for it is obvious that if only what illustrates the country and its life *in a distinctive way* be chosen, the subjective and unlocal literature must be necessarily passed over, entraining the omission of most of the poems whose merit lies in perfection of finish. It is therefore greatly to be desired that a purely literary anthology may soon be brought together by some one. Such a collection was made in 1867, in the Rev. Edward Hartley Dewart's "Selections." Two or three other partial collections have been made, the best being Seranus' "Canadian Birthday Book," which affords a miniature survey of the chief verse-writers, both French and English. The most remarkable point of difference between the selections of Dewart and the poetry which has followed, is the tone of exultation and confidence which the singers have assumed since Confederation, for up to that epoch the verse was apologetic and depressed. Everything now points hopefully. Not only is the poetry more confident, but far better. A good deal of the best verse in American magazines is written in Canada.

The order of this collection is in sections, treating of the Imperial Spirit, the New Nationality, the Indian, the *Voyageur* and *Habitant*, Settlement Life, Sports and Free Life, Historical Incidents, Places, and Seasons. They give merely, it should be understood, a sketch of the range of the subjects. Canadian history, for example, as any one acquainted with Parkman will know, perfectly teems with noble deeds and great events, of which only a small share have been sung, whereof there is only space here for a much smaller share. The North-West and British Columbia, that Pacific clime of charm—the gold-diggings Province, land of salmon rivers, and of the Douglas firs which hide daylight at noonday—have been scarcely sung at all, owing to their newness. The poetry of the Winter Carnival, splendid scenic spectacle of gay Northern arts and delights, is only rudimentary also. Those who have been present at the thrilling spectacle of the nocturnal storming of the Ice Palace in Montreal, when the whole city, dressing itself in the picturesque snow-shoe costume and arraying its streets in lights and colours, rises as one man in a tumultuous enthusiasm, must feel that something of a future lies before the poetry of these strange and wonderful elements.

To omit a bow to the French would be ungracious. In the larger form of this work in the Windsor Series, we have devoted a special appendix to *ipsis verbis* specimens of Chauveau, Sulte, Fréchette, and Le May, leaders who have been very highly honoured in France.

In concluding, I desire to express my sense of shortcoming in the work, but believe it will be generally admitted that I have spared no necessary trouble.

Both Editors regret to say that, through an accidental cause unnecessary to explain, more MSS. were sent to the publishers than the volume required. As no time could be lost, the General Editor had no recourse except to undertake the difficult task of cutting down the matter, which he did in accordance with his best judgment, but guided by the sole criterion of the symmetry of the work. Some good poetry originally included has not found a place, owing to the necessary reduction, and apology is tendered where unintentional injustice has resulted.

And now, the canoes are packed, our *voyageurs* are waiting for us, the paddles are ready, let us start!

W. D. L.

I.—The Imperial Spirit.

Canadian Poems and Lays.

I.—THE IMPERIAL SPIRIT.

HASTINGS.

JOHN READE.

I.

OCTOBER's woods are bright and gay, a thousand colours vie
To win the golden smiles the Sun sends gleaming thro' the sky;
And tho' the flowers are dead and gone, one garden seems the earth,
For, in God's world, as one charm dies, another starts to birth.

II.

To every season is its own peculiar beauty given,
In every age of mortal men we see the Hand of Heaven;

And century to century utters a glorious speech,
And peace to war, and war to peace, eternal lessons teach.

III.

O grand old woods, your forest-sires were thus as bright and gay,
Before the axe's murderous voice had spoiled their sylvan play;
When other axes smote our sires, and laid them stiff and low,
On Hastings' unforgotten field, *eight hundred years ago.*

IV.

Eight hundred years ago, long years, before Jacques Cartier clomb
The Royal Height, where now no more the red men fearless roam!
Eight hundred years ago, long years, before Columbus came
From stately Spain to find the world that ought to bear his name!

V.

The Sussex woods were bright and red on that October morn;
And Sussex soil was red with blood before the next was born;
But from that red united clay another race did start
On the great stage of destiny to act a noble part.

VI.

So God doth mould, as pleaseth Him, the nations of His choice;
Now, in the battle-cry is heard His purifying voice

And now, with Orphic strains of peace he draws to
    nationhood
The scattered tribes that dwell apart by mountain, sea,
    and wood.

VII.

He took the lonely poet Celt, and taught him Roman
    lore;
Then from the wealds of Saxony He brought the sons of
    Thor;
Next from his craggy home the Dane came riding o'er
    the sea;
And last, came William with his bands of Norman
    chivalry.

VIII.

And now, as our young nationhood is struggling into
    birth,
God grant its infant pulse may beat with our forefathers'
    worth!
And, as we gather into *one*, let us recall with pride
That we are of the blood of those who fought when
    Harold died.

CANADA TO ENGLAND.[1]

ANONYMOUS.

Mother of many prosperous lands,
  Thy children in this far-off West,—
Seeing that vague and undefined
  A cloud comes up to mar our rest ;
Fearing that busy tongues, whose speech
Is mischief, may have caused a breach,
And frayed the delicate links which bind
  Our people each to each,—
With loving hearts and outstretched hands
  Send greeting leal and kind.

Heed not the teachings of a school
Of shallow sophists who would part
The outlying members of thy rule ;
  Who fain would lop, with felon stroke,
  The branches of our English oak,
And, wronging the great English heart,
  Would deem her honour cheaply sold
For higher prices on the mart,
  And increased hoard of gold.

What though a many thousand miles
  Of boisterous waters ebb and flow
Between us and the favoured Isles,—
  The "inviolate Isles" which boast thy sway !

---

[1] Appeared in *New Dominion Monthly*, 1869, with a statement that it had had a wide circulation "some years ago." Internal evidence shows it to have been written about 1861.

No time nor distance can divide
What gentlest bonds have firmest tied ;
And this we fain would have thee know,
  The which let none gainsay.
Nay rather, let the wide world hear
That we so far are yet so near,
That, come what may, in weal or woe,
  Our hearts are one this day.

Thus late, when death's cold wings were spread,
  And when the nation's eyes were dim,
We also bowed the stricken head,
We too the eloquent teardrops shed
  In heartfelt grief for *him*.

. . . . . .

When recent danger threatened near,
  We nerved our hearts to play our part;
Not making boast, nor feeling fear;
  But as the news of insult spread
    Were none to dally or to lag;
For all the grand old Island spirit
Which Britain's chivalrous sons inherit
    Was roused, and as one heart, one head,
      We rallied round our flag.

And now as then unchanged, the same
  Though filling each our separate spheres;
Thy joys, thy griefs, and thy good name
  Are ours, and or in good or ill ;
Our pride of race we have not lost,
And aye it is our loftiest boast
  That we are Britons still !
And in the gradual lapse of years

We look, that 'neath these distant skies
Another England shall arise,—
  A noble scion of the old,—
Still to herself and lineage true,
  And prizing honour more than gold.
This is *our* hope, and as for you,
  Be just as you are generous, mother,
And let not those who rashly speak
Things that they know not, render weak
  The ties that bind us to each other.

EMPIRE FIRST.

POPULAR SONG.

JOHN TALON-LESPÉRANCE—"LACLÈDE."

SHALL we break the plight of youth,
  And pledge us to an alien love?
No! We hold our faith and truth,
  Trusting to the God above.
    Stand, Canadians, firmly stand,
    Round the flag of Fatherland.

Britain bore us in our flank,
  Britain nursed us at our birth,
Britain reared us to our rank
  'Mid the nations of the earth.
    Stand, Canadians, etc.

In the hour of pain and dread,
  In the gathering of the storm,
Britain raised above our head
  Her broad shield and sheltering arm.
    Stand, Canadians, etc.

O triune kingdom of the brave,
  O sea-girt Island of the free,
O empire of the land and wave,
  Our hearts, our hands, are all for thee.
    Stand, Canadians, etc.

THE CANADIANS ON THE NILE.

William Wye Smith.

O, THE East is but the West, with the sun a little hotter;
And the pine becomes a palm, by the dark Egyptian
    water :
And the Nile's like many a stream we know, that fills its
    brimming cup,—
We'll think it is the Ottawa, as we track the batteaux
    up !
    Pull, pull, pull ! as we track the batteaux up !
    It's easy shooting homeward, when we're at the
      top !

O, the cedar and the spruce line each dark Canadian
    river;
But the thirsty date is here, where the sultry sunbeams
    quiver;

And the mocking mirage spreads its view, afar on either
    hand;
But strong we bend the sturdy oar, towards the Southern
    land!
        Pull, pull, pull! as we track the batteaux up!
        It's easy shooting homeward, when we're at the
            top!

O, we've tracked the Rapids up, and o'er many a portage
    crossing;
And it's often such we've seen, though so loud the waves
    are tossing!
Then, it's homeward when the run is o'er! o'er stream,
    and ocean deep—
To bring the memory of the Nile, where the maple
    shadows sleep!
        Pull, pull, pull! as we track the batteaux up!
        It's easy shooting homeward, when we're at the
            top!

And it yet may come to pass, that the hearts and hands
    so ready
May be sought again to help, when some poise is off the
    steady!
And the Maple and the Pine be matched, with British
    Oak the while,
As once beneath Egyptian suns, the Canadians on the
    Nile!
        Pull, pull, pull! as we track the batteaux up!
        It's easy shooting homeward, when we're at the
            top!

II.—THE NEW NATIONALITY.

II.—THE NEW NATIONALITY.

DOMINION DAY.

"FIDELIS."

With *feu-de-joie* and merry bells, and cannon's thundering peal,
And pennons fluttering on the breeze, and serried rows of steel,
We greet, again, the birthday morn of our young giant's land,
From the Atlantic stretching wide to far Pacific strand;
With flashing rivers, ocean lakes, and prairies wide and free,
And waterfalls, and forests dim, and mountains by the sea;
A country on whose birth-hour smiled the genius of romance,
Above whose cradle brave hands waved the lily-cross of France;
Whose infancy was grimly nursed in peril, pain, and woe;
Whose gallant hearts found early graves beneath Canadian snow;

When savage raid and ambuscade and famine's sore
    distress,
Combined their strength, in vain, to crush the dauntless
    French *noblesse;*
When her dim, trackless forest lured, again and yet
    again,
From silken courts of sunny France, her flower, the
    brave Champlain.
And now, her proud traditions boast four blazoned rolls
    of fame,—
Crecy's and Flodden's deadly foes our ancestors we
    claim;
Past feud and battle buried far behind the peaceful years,
While Gaul and Celt and Briton turn to pruning-hooks
    their spears;
Four nations welded into one,—with long historic past,
Have found, in these our western wilds, one common
    life, at last;
Through the young giant's mighty limbs, that stretch
    from sea to sea,
There runs a throb of conscious life—of waking energy.
From Nova Scotia's misty coast to far Columbia's
    shore,
She wakes,—a band of scattered homes and colonies no
    more,
But a young nation, with her life full beating in her
    breast,
A noble future in her eyes—the Britain of the West.
Hers be the noble task to fill the yet untrodden plains
With fruitful, many-sided life that courses through her
    veins;
The English honour, nerve, and pluck,—the Scotsman's
    love of right,—
The grace and courtesy of France,—the Irish fancy
    bright,—

The Saxon's faithful love of home, and home's affections
    blest;
And, chief of all, our holy faith,—of all our treasures
    best.
A people poor in pomp and state, but rich in noble
    deeds,
Holding that righteousness exalts the people that it
    leads;
As yet the waxen mould is soft, the opening page is fair;
It rests with those who rule us now, to leave their
    impress there,—
The stamp of true nobility, high honour, stainless truth;
The earnest quest of noble ends; the generous heart of
    youth;
The love of country, soaring far above dull party strife;
The love of learning, art, and song—the crowning grace
    of life;
The love of science, soaring far through Nature's hidden
    ways;
The love and fear of Nature's God—a nation's highest
    praise.
So, in the long hereafter, this Canada shall be
The worthy heir of British power and British liberty;
Spreading the blessings of her sway to her remotest
    bounds,
While, with the fame of her fair name, a continent
    resounds.
True to her high traditions, to Britain's ancient glory
Of patient saint and martyr, alive in deathless story;
Strong, in their liberty and truth, to shed from shore to
    shore
A light among the nations, till nations are no more.

CANADA.

Charles G. D. Roberts.

O Child of Nations, giant-limbed,
    Who stand'st among the nations now
Unheeded, unadorned, unhymned,
    With unanointed brow,—

How long the ignoble sloth, how long
    The trust in greatness not thine own?
Surely the lion's brood is strong
    To front the world alone!

How long the indolence, ere thou dare
    Achieve thy destiny, seize thy fame,—
Ere our proud eyes behold thee bear
    A nation's franchise, nation's name?

The Saxon force, the Celtic fire,
    These are thy manhood's heritage!
Why rest with babes and slaves? Seek higher
    The place of race and age.

I see to every wind unfurled
    The flag that bears the Maple-Wreath;
Thy swift keels furrow round the world
    Its blood-red folds beneath;

Thy swift keels cleave the furthest seas;
    Thy white sails swell with alien gales;
To stream on each remotest breeze
    The black smoke of thy pipes exhales.

O Falterer, let thy past convince
   Thy future,—all the growth, the gain,
The fame since Cartier knew thee, since
   Thy shores beheld Champlain.

Montcalm and Wolfe! Wolfe and Montcalm!
   Quebec, thy storied citadel
Attest in burning song and psalm
   How here thy heroes fell!

O Thou that bor'st the battle's brunt
   At Queenston, and at Lundy's Lane,—
On whose scant ranks but iron front
   The battle broke in vain!—

Whose was the danger, whose the day,
   From whose triumphant throats the cheers,
At Chrysler's Farm, at Chateauguay,
   Storming like clarion-bursts our ears?

On soft Pacific slopes,—beside
   Strange floods that northward rave and fall,—
Where chafes Acadia's chainless tide—
   Thy sons await thy call.

They await; but some in exile, some
   With strangers housed, in stranger lands;—
And some Canadian lips are dumb
   Beneath Egyptian sands.

O mystic Nile! Thy secret yields
   Before us; thy most ancient dreams
Are mixed with far Canadian fields
   And murmur of Canadian streams.

But thou, my Country, dream not thou !
  Wake, and behold how night is done,—
How on thy breast, and o'er thy brow,
  Bursts the uprising sun !

THE CONFUSED DAWN.

W. D. LIGHTHALL.

YOUNG MAN.

WHAT are the Vision and the Cry
That haunt the new Canadian soul?
  Dim grandeur spreads we know not why
O'er mountain, forest, tree, and knoll,
  And murmurs indistinctly fly.—
  Some magic moment sure is nigh.
O Seer, the curtain roll !

SEER.

The Vision, mortal, it is this—
  Dead mountain, forest, knoll, and tree
Awaken all endued with bliss,
  A native land—O think !—to be—
Thy native land—and ne'er amiss,
Its smile shall like a lover's kiss
  From henceforth seem to thee.

The Cry thou couldst not understand,
  Which runs through that new realm of light,

From Breton's to Vancouver's strand
  O'er many a lovely landscape bright,
It is their waking utterance grand,
The great refrain, "A NATIVE LAND!"
  Thine be the ear, the sight.

FROM "'85."

BARRY STRATON.

SHALL we not all be one race, shaping and welding the nation?
  Is not our country too broad for the schisms which shake petty lands?
Yea, we shall join in our might, and keep sacred our firm Federation,
  Shoulder to shoulder arrayed, hearts open to hearts, hands to hands!

CANADA NOT LAST.

W. D. LIGHTHALL.

AT VENICE.

Lo! Venice, gay with colour, lights, and song,
  Calls from St. Mark's with ancient voice and strange:
I am the Witch of Cities! glide along
  My silver streets that never wear by change

Of years; forget the years, and pain, and wrong,
And every sorrow reigning men among;
   Know I can soothe thee, please and marry thee
To my illusions. Old, and siren-strong,
   I smile immortal, while the mortals flee
Who whiten on to death in wooing me!

AT FLORENCE.

Say, what more fair, by Arno's bridgèd gleam,[1]
   Than Florence, viewed from San Miniato's slope
At eventide, when west along the stream
   The last of day reflects a silver hope!—
Lo! all else softened in the twilight beam:—
The city's mass blent in one hazy cream;
   The brown Dome 'midst it, and the Lily Tower,
And stern Old Tower more near, and hills that seem
   Afar, like clouds to fade, and hills of power
   On this side, greenly dark with cypress, vine, and bower!

AT ROME.

End of desire to stray I feel would come,
   Though Italy were all fair skies to me,
Though France's fields went mad with flowery foam,
   And Blanc put on a special majesty.
Not all could match the growing thought of home,
Nor tempt to exile. Look I not on ROME,—
   This ancient, modern, mediæval queen,—
Yet still sigh westward over hill and dome,
   Imperial ruin, and villa's princely scene,
   Lovely with pictured saints and marble gods serene!

---

[1] "Sovra'l bel fiume d'Arno la gran villa."—DANTE.

REFLECTION.

Rome, Florence, Venice,—noble, fair, and quaint,
   They reign in robes of magic round me here;
But fading blotted, dim, a picture faint,
   With spell more silent, only pleads a tear.
Plead not! Thou hast my heart, O picture dim!
   I see the fields, I see the autumn hand
Of God upon the maples! Answer Him
   With weird, translucent glories, ye that stand
Like spirits in scarlet and in amethyst!
I see the sun break over you; the mist
    On hills that lift from iron bases grand
    Their heads superb!—the dream, it is my native land!

COLLECT FOR DOMINION DAY.

Charles G. D. Roberts.

Father of Nations! Help of the feeble hand,
   Strength of the strong! to whom the nations kneel!
Stay and destroyer, at whose just command
   Earth's kingdoms tremble and her empires reel!
Who dost the low uplift, the small make great,
   And dost abase the ignorantly proud;
Of our scant people mould a mighty state,
   To the strong stern, to Thee in meekness bowed!
Father of unity, make this people one!
   Weld, interfuse them in the patriot's flame,—
Whose forging on Thine anvil was begun
   In blood late shed to purge the common shame;
That so our hearts, the fever of faction done,
   Banish old feud in our young nation's name.

III.—The Indian.

III.—THE INDIAN.

A BLOOD-RED RING HUNG ROUND THE MOON.

"Barry Dane"—John E. Logan.

A BLOOD-RED ring hung round the moon,
    Hung round the moon.   Ah me! Ah me!
I heard the piping of the Loon,
    A wounded Loon.   Ah me!
And yet the eagle feathers rare,
I, trembling, wove in my brave's hair.

He left me in the early morn,
    The early morn.   Ah me! Ah me!
The feathers swayed like stately corn,[1]
    So like the corn.   Ah me!
A fierce wind swept across the plain,
The stately corn was snapt in twain.

[1] "Indian corn" is maize.

They crushed in blood the hated race,
  The hated race. Ah me! Ah me!
I only clasped a cold, blind face,
  His cold, dead face. Ah me!
A blood-red ring hangs in my sight,
I hear the Loon cry every night.

THE DEPARTING OF CLOTE SCARP.

CHARLES G. D. ROBERTS.

IT is so long ago; and men well-nigh
Forget what gladness was, and how the earth
Gave corn in plenty, and the rivers fish,
And the woods meat, before he went away.
His going was on this wise.

                      All the works
And words and ways of men and beasts became
Evil, and all their thoughts continually
Were but of evil. Then he made a feast.
Upon the shore that is beside the sea
That takes the setting sun, he ordered it,
And called the beasts thereto. Only the men
He called not, seeing them evil utterly.
He fed the panther's crafty brood, and filled
The lean wolf's hunger; from the hollow tree
His honey stayed the bear's terrific jaws;
And the brown rabbit couched at peace, within
The circling shadow of the eagle's wings.

And when the feast was done, he told them all
That now, because their ways were evil grown,
On that same day he must depart from them,
And they should look upon his face no more.
Then all the beasts were very sorrowful.
It was near sunset, and the wind was still,
And down the yellow shore a thin wave washed
Slowly; and Clote Scarp launched his birch canoe,
And spread his yellow sail, and moved from shore,
Though no wind followed, streaming in the sail,
Or roughening the clear waters after him.
And all the beasts stood by the shore, and watched.
Then to the west appeared a long red trail
Over the wave; and Clote Scarp sailed and sang
Till the canoe grew little like a bird,
And black, and vanished in the shining trail.
And when the beasts could see his form no more,
They still could hear him, singing as he sailed,
And still they listened, hanging down their heads
In long row, where the thin wave washed and fled.
But when the sound of singing died, and when
They lifted up their voices in their grief,
Lo! on the mouth of every beast a strange
New tongue! Then rose they all and fled apart,
Nor met again in council from that day.

From "TECUMSEH."—Act I., Scene 2.

Charles Mair.

LEFROY.

This region is as lavish of its flowers
As Heaven of its primrose blooms by night.

This is the Arum, which within its root
Folds life and death; and this the Prince's Pine,
Fadeless as love and truth—the fairest form
That ever sun-shower washed with sudden rain.
This golden cradle is the Moccasin Flower,
Wherein the Indian hunter sees his hound;
And this dark chalice is the Pitcher-Plant,
Stored with the water of forgetfulness.
Whoever drinks of it, whose heart is pure,
Will sleep for aye 'neath foodful asphodel,
And dream of endless love.

. . . . . .

There was a time on this fair continent
When all things throve in spacious peacefulness.
The prosperous forests unmolested stood,
For where the stalwart oak grew there it lived
Long ages, and then died among its kind.
The hoary pines—those ancients of the earth—
Brimful of legends of the early world,
Stood thick on their own mountains unsubdued.
And all things else illumined by the sun,
Inland or by the lifted wave, had rest.
The passionate or calm pageants of the skies
No artist drew; but in the auburn west

Innumerable faces of fair cloud
Vanished in silent darkness with the day.
The prairie realm—vast ocean's paraphrase—
Rich in wild grasses numberless, and flowers
Unnamed save in mute Nature's inventory,
No civilised barbarian trenched for gain.
And all that flowed was sweet and uncorrupt.
The rivers and their tributary streams,
Undammed, wound on for ever, and gave up
Their lonely torrents to weird gulfs of sea,
And ocean wastes unshadowed by a sail.
And all the wild life of this western world
Knew not the fear of man; yet in those woods,
And by those plenteous streams and mighty lakes,
And on stupendous steppes of peerless plain,
And in the rocky gloom of canyons deep,
Screened by the stony ribs of mountains hoar
Which steeped their snowy peaks in purging cloud,
And down the continent where tropic suns
Warmed to her very heart the mother earth,
And in the congeal'd north where silence self
Ached with intensity of stubborn frost,
There lived a soul more wild than barbarous;
A tameless soul—the sunburnt savage free—
Free and untainted by the greed of gain,
Great Nature's man, content with Nature's food.

THE ARCTIC INDIAN'S FAITH.

Thomas D'Arcy M'Gee.

We worship the Spirit that walks unseen
    Through our land of ice and snow;
We know not His face, we know not His place,
    But His presence and power we know.

Does the Buffalo need the Pale-face word
    To find his pathway far?
What guide has he to the hidden ford,
    Or where the green pastures are?
Who teacheth the Moose that the hunter's gun
    Is peering out of the shade?
Who teacheth the doe and the fawn to run
    In the track the Moose has made?

Him do we follow, Him do we fear,
    The Spirit of earth and sky;
Who hears with the *Wapiti's* eager ear
    His poor red children's cry;
Whose whisper we note in every breeze
    That stirs the birch canoe;
Who hangs the reindeer-moss on the trees
    For the food of the Caribou.

The Spirit we worship, who walks unseen
    Through our land of ice and snow;
We know not His face, we know not His place,
    But His presence and power we know.

THE CAUGHNAWAGA BEADWORK-SELLER.

W. D. LIGHTHALL.

Kanawaki,—"By the Rapid,"—
　Low the sunset 'midst thee lies;
And from the wild Reservation
　Evening's breeze begins to rise.
Faint the Konoronkwa chorus
　Drifts across the currents strong;
Spirit-like the parish steeple
　Stands thine ancient walls among.

Kanawaki,—"By the Rapid,"—
　How the sun amidst thee burns!
Village of the Praying Nation,
　Thy dark child to thee returns.
All day through the pale-faced city,
　Silent, selling beaded wares,
I have wandered with my basket,
　Lone, excepting for their stares.

They are white men; we are Indians;
　What a gulf their stares proclaim!
They are mounting; we are dying:
　All our heritage they claim.
We are dying, dwindling, dying!
　Strait and smaller grows our bound:
They are mounting up to heaven,
　And are pressing all around.

Thou art ours,—little remnant,
　Ours from countless thousand years,—
Part of the old Indian world:
　Thy breath from far the Indian cheers.

Back to thee, O Kanawâki !
  Let the rapids dash between
Indian homes and white men's manners,—
  Kanawâki and Lachine !

O, my dear ! O Knife-and-Arrows !
  Thou art bronzed, thy limbs are lithe ;
How I laugh when through the crosse-game
  Slipst thou like red elder-withe !
Thou art none of these pale-faces !
  When with thee I'll happy feel ;
For thou art the Indian warrior
  From thy head unto thy heel !

Sweet the Kōnoronkwa chorus
  Floats across the currents strong ;
Clear behold the parish steeple
  Rise the ancient walls among !
Skim us deftly, noiseless paddle :
  In my shawl my bosom burns !
Kanawâki,—" By the Rapid,"—
  Thy own child to thee returns.

WAHONOMIN.[1] (INDIAN HYMN TO THE QUEEN.)

FREDERICK GEORGE SCOTT.

GREAT mother ! we have wondered that thy sons,
Thy pale sons, should have left thy side and come
To these wild plains, and sought the haunts of bears
And red men. Why their battle with the woods?

[1] "Wahonomin" is an Indian cry of lamentation.

Whither go they upon the gods of iron,
Out of the golden sunrise to the mists
Of purple evening in the setting west?
Their lives have scarce as many moons as ours,
Nor happier are. We know not what they seek;
For death's cold finger chills their fevered life,
As in the wilds he stills the meanest worm,
And death flies with them over all their paths,
And waits them in the heart of wildest waste;
They cannot break his power. Forgive these thoughts
If, as they rise like mists, they dim the gold
That zones thy brow. They came to us at night,
As we have sat in council round the fire;
They seemed the echo of the sighing pines
Far in our soul. One evening rose a chief,
White-headed, bowed with years, one hand on staff,
One on death's arm, preparing for the way.
"My sons," he said, "these people are not wise,
We bide our time, and they will pass away;
Then shall the red man come like a bird in spring,
And build the broken camp, and hunt and fish
In his old woods. These people pass away;
For I have thought through many nights and days,
And wondered what they seek; and now I know,
And knowing, say these people are not wise.
They found these plains beneath the burning west,
And westward, ever westward, still they press,
Seeking the shining meadows of the land
Where the sun sleeps, and, folded 'neath his wings,
The happy spirits breathe eternal day.
But I have lived thro' fivescore changing years,
And I have talked with wintry-headed chiefs,
And I have heard that kingdom is not reached
Thro' woods and plains, but by the bridge of death.
This people is not wise; we bide our time."

CAUGHNAWAGA SONG.

(*Rinonwes, rinonwes, Rakeni.*)

Tr. JOHN WANIENTE JOCKS.

CHORUS.

I love him, I love him, father,—
That young man!

MAIDEN.

Well, father, what is thy word?
My spirit is now to marry.

FATHER.

Ashamed be thou, my child,—
Thou whom I hold my little one,—
Thou are yet too young;
Thou can'st not get thee thy food.

MAIDEN (*in the words of the Chorus*).

I love him, I love him, father,—
That young man.

FATHER.

Hard drinks he, he thou lovest;
Great tears this would later make thee shed.

CHORUS (*passionately*).

I love him, I love him, father,—
That young man.

FATHER.

Thou askest for food; he will show thee a
    bottle.

CHORUS (*softly*).

Yet I love him, I love him, father,—
That young man.

IV.—THE VOYAGEUR AND HABITANT.

IV.—THE VOYAGEUR AND HABITANT.

THE OLD RÉGIME.

(*From "Song of Welcome."*)

"Seranus."

Yet survives a strain,
　One of saddest singing,
Chant of Habitant,
　On the river ringing;
Born in olden France,
All of dame and dance,
　Brought with golden lily.
From the distant pines,
From the northern waters,
From hardy sons and toiling daughters,
　Salutation; Salutation!

RECIT.

Strange visions of a land beyond the sea,
The quaint old towns and farms of Normandy,—
The land he never saw and ne'er will see!

Strange visions of a life as bright and gay
As his own now is quiet, dull and gray,—
The many-coloured life of Yesterday!

Strange visions of a past still dimly dear,
Since he, the toiler, cannot but revere
The past he may not see, nor feel, nor hear!

And strange for us the other sudden thought,
How without dreams that float across the foam
Of gray Atlantic, float, and float, and flash
At length on shores of Gallic name and fame
Into the actual glitter of old time—
We hold among our best possessions still,
E'en here in new and northern land—a past,
We have not many ruins, it is true;
And those we have, pray daily, but in vain,
For friendly green that grows not *gratis* here.
Not more than scraps of history, they have said!
They are enough to interest, kindle too,
If wisely we have learned to love our land,
But not enough to bore—no pedants here.
Here—tower and trophy, mound and monument,
The cairn and cuneiform of an Old World
Give place to Nature in her purity.
But what we have, we cling to. We would keep
All dear tradition; be it picturesque
In the old *voyageur* with gay festoons

Of floating ribbons, happy, noisy, free;
Or polished, in the careful cavalier,
Fresh-furbelowed from out his sunny France,—
Heroic, in the story of Verchères;
Or dark, in that of dismal Beaumanoir.
Through the long years we see as in a dream,—
And will not part with it—the Old Régime.

Powdered tresses and rich brocade,
Stately matron and charming maid;

Flashing steel and stubborn rust,
Blood for blood and thrust for thrust;

Hand on heart in the good old style,
Courtly lips on lips without guile;

The young sweet land of *La Nouvelle France*,
Knew it all by a strange sweet chance;

All the charm of the dainty dressing,
All the force of a gay professing.

CHORUS.—And still we seem
      As in a dream,
      To watch the Old Régime,
      The Old Régime!

Crowned Quebec on her Citadel
Fierce wild tales of her youth can tell;

Tales of ghosts that still pursue
Scenes of riot and bloodshed too;

Tales of dark stains on the flooring,
Tales of woman's wild imploring ;

The young sweet land of *La Nouvelle France*,
Had its share of Old World romance ;

But sobered by Time are sword and gown,
And quiet reigns in the grey old town.

CHORUS.—Yet still we seem
   As in a dream,
   To watch the Old Régime,
   The Old Régime !

MALBROUCK.

(*Old Chanson.*)

Tr. WILLIAM M'LENNAN.

MALBROUCK has gone a-fighting,
Mironton, mironton, mirontaine,
Malbrouck has gone a-fighting
But when will he return ?

Perchance he'll come at Easter
Or else at Trinity Term.

But Trinity Term is over
And Malbrouck comes not yet.

My Lady climbs her watch tower
As high as she can get.

She sees her page approaching
All clad in sable hue:

" Ah page, brave page, what tidings
From my true lord bring you ? "

" The news I bring, fair Lady,
Will make your tears run down ;

" Put off your rose-red dress so fine
And doff your satin gown ;

" Monsieur Malbrouck is dead, alas !
And buried too, for aye ;

" I saw four officers who bore
His mighty corse away.

" One bore his cuirass, and his friend
His shield of iron wrought ;

" The third his mighty sabre bore,
And the fourth—he carried nought.

" And at the corners of his tomb
They planted rose-marie ;

"And from their tops the nightingale
Rings out her carol free.

"We saw, above the laurels,
His soul fly forth amain;

"And each one fell upon his face
And then rose up again.

"And so we sang the glories
For which great Malbrouck bled;

"And when the whole was ended
Each one went off to bed.

"I say no more my Lady,
 Mironton, mironton, mirontaine,
I say no more, my Lady,
As nought more can be said."

À LA CLAIRE FONTAINE.

(*Old Chanson.*)

Tr. W. D. LIGHTHALL.

I.

UNTO the crystal fountain
 For pleasure did I stray;
So fair I found the waters
 My limbs in them I lay.

Long is it I have loved thee,
Thee shall I love alway,
   My dearest ;
Long is it I have loved thee,
Thee shall I love alway.

II.

So fair I found the waters,
 My limbs in them I lay ;
Beneath an oak tree resting,
 I heard a roundelay.
   Long is it, etc.

III.

Beneath an oak tree resting,
 I heard a roundelay,
The nightingale was singing
 On the oak tree's topmost spray.
   Long is it, etc.

IV.

The nightingale was singing
 On the oak tree's topmost spray :—
Sing, nightingale, keep singing,
 Thou who hast heart so gay !
   Long is it, etc.

V.

Sing, nightingale, keep singing,
 Thou hast a heart so gay,
Thou hast a heart so merry,
 While mine is sorrow's prey.
   Long is it, etc.

VI.

For I have lost my mistress,
  Whom I did true obey,
All for a bunch of roses,
  Whereof I said her nay.
              Long is it, etc.

VII.

I would those luckless roses
  Were on their bush to-day,
And that itself the rosebush
  Were plunged in ocean's spray.

Long is it I have loved thee,
Thee shall I love alway,
        My dearest ;
Long is it I have loved thee,
Thee shall I love alway.

EN ROULANT MA BOULÉ.

(Old Chanson.)

Tr. WILLIAM M'LENNAN.

BEHIND the Manor lies the mere,
  En roulant ma boulé ;
Three ducks bathe in its waters clear,
  En roulant ma boulé.

Rouli, roulant, ma boulé roulant,
En roulant ma boulé roulant,
En roulant ma boulé.

Three fairy ducks swim without fear:
The Prince goes hunting far and near.

The Prince at last draws near the lake;
He bears his gun of magic make.

With magic gun of silver bright,
He sights the Black but kills the White.

He sights the Black but kills the White:
Ah! cruel Prince, my heart you smite.

Ah! cruel Prince, my heart you break,
In killing thus my snow-white Drake.

My snow-white Drake, my Love, my King;
The crimson life-blood stains his wing.

His life-blood falls in rubies bright,
His diamond eyes have lost their light.

The cruel ball has found its quest,
His golden bill sinks on his breast.

His golden bill sinks on his breast,
His plumes go floating East and West.

Far, far they're borne to distant lands,
Till gathered by fair maidens' hands;

Till gathered by fair maidens' hands;
And form at last a soldier's bed.

And form at last a soldier's bed,
  En roulant ma boulé ;
Sweet refuge for the wanderer's head,
  En roulant ma boulé.

  Rouli, roulant, ma boulé roulant,
  En roulant ma boulé roulant,
  En roulant ma boulé.

ENTRE PARIS ET SAINT-DENIS.

(*Old Chanson.*)

Tr. WILLIAM M'LENNAN.

TWIXT Paris fair and St. Denis
The dance was up one day,
And all the ladies of the town
Looked on in brave array.

  Sur la feuille ron, . . . don don don,
  Sur la joli', joli' feuille ronde.

And all the ladies of the town
Looked on in brave array,
All save the Princess fair, who glanced
Adown the dusty way.

The Princess fair cast wistful looks
Adown the dusty way,
And soon she saw her messenger
Ride from where Nantés lay.

She saw her faithful messenger
His way from Nantés wing;
"Now, messenger, from Nantés town
What tidings do you bring?"

"Now, Messenger, bold Messenger,
What news from Nantés fair?"
"The only news I bring, fair Dame,
Your lover bade me bear.

"The only news I bring is this:
Your lover bade me say,
That he has found a sweetheart new,
Choose you a gallant gay.

"Choose you another gallant gay,
For I've a sweetheart rare,"
"Now is she wiser far than I,
Or is her face more fair?"

"Now is she wiser far than I,
Or is her face more fair?"
"Although not near so fair as you,
Her wisdom's past compare.

"Her beauty is not like to yours,
But secret lore she knows;
She makes the snow, she makes the hail,
She makes the wind that blows.

"She makes the wind that blows so free,
She makes the snow so fine;
At midnight hour, within her bower,
She makes the sun to shine.

"She makes the sun to shine again
At midnight in her bower;
And on the borders of the sea
Makes rosemary to flower."
   Sur la feuille ron, . . . don don don,
   Sur la joli', joli' feuille ronde.

MARIANSON.

(Old Chanson.)

Tr. WILLIAM M'LENNAN.

"Ah! Marianson, my beauteous dame,
Where is your lord and master gone?"

"My lord rides to the battle-plain,
I know not if he'll come again."

"Ah! Marianson, my lady fair,
Lend me your rings of gold so rare."

"In the iron chest beside my bed,
You'll find the rings," she sweetly said.

"Now, Goldsmith, fashion me with care
Three golden rings of metal rare.

Three golden rings of fashion rare,
Like those that Marianson doth wear."

When he receives his golden rings
Upon his steed he lightly springs.

The first he meets upon the road
Is Marianson's haughty lord.

"Fair greeting now, bold cavalier,
What tidings do you bring me here?"

"Of tidings new I bring you none,
Save of the Lady Marianson."

"Ah! Marianson, my lady fair!
She's faithful aye, I'll boldly swear."

"I say not 'yes,'—I say not 'no,'
But see—the rings from her hands of snow."

"You lie! you lie! bold cavalier;
My wife is faithful, far or near."

His wife stood on the ramparts high;
She saw her lord ride wildly by.

Her heart stood still with a sudden fear
When she marked his face as he drew anear.

"Now, mother, show our new-born child,
Its grace will calm his anger wild."

"My son, behold your son and heir;
What name wilt thou give the babe to bear?"

He cried, "I'll give the child a name
That will fill its mother's life with shame."

He has seized the infant in its mirth,
And thrice has dashed it to the earth.

And Marianson, that lady fair,
He has tied to his horse by her golden hair.

Three days, three nights, he rode like wind,
And never cast a look behind.

Till, at close of the third long night,
He turned and looked on that awful sight.

" Ah ! Marianson, my lady fair,
Where are your golden rings so rare ? "

" In the iron chest, beside my bed,
You'll find the rings," she sadly said.

He has ta'en the keys with an evil grace,
And has found the rings in their hiding-place.

" Ah ! Marianson, my lady fair,
You shall have the best chirurgeon's care."

" The best chirurgeon I would crave
Is a fine white sheet for my quiet grave."

" Ah ! Marianson, my beauteous dame,
Will God e'er pardon all my shame ? "

" My death is pardoned now," she smiled,
" But never that of our helpless child."

THE RE-SETTLEMENT OF ACADIA.

Arthur Wentworth Eaton.

The rocky slopes for emerald had changed their garb of gray,
When the vessels from Connecticut came sailing up the bay,
There were flashing lights on every wave that drew the strangers on,
And wreaths of wild arbutus round the brows of Blomidon.

Five years in desolation the Acadian land had lain,
Five golden harvest moons had wooed the fallow fields in vain;
Five times the winter snows caressed, and summer sunsets smiled,
On lonely clumps of willows, and fruit trees growing wild.

There was silence in the forest, and along the Uniac shore,
And not a habitation from Canard to Beauséjour,
But many a ruined cellar and many a broken wall
Told the story of Acadia's prosperity, and fall!

And even in the sunshine of that peaceful day in June,
When Nature swept her harp, and found the strings in perfect tune,
The land seemed calling wildly for its owners, far away,
The exiles scattered on the coast from Maine to Charleston Bay.

Where, with many bitter longings for their fair homes and
    their dead,
They bowed their heads in anguish, and would not be
    comforted;
And like the Jewish exiles, long ago, beyond the sea,
They could not sing the songs of home in their captivity!

But the simple Norman peasant-folk shall till the land no
    more,
For the vessels from Connecticut have anchored by the
    shore,
And many a sturdy Puritan, his mind with Scripture
    stored,
Rejoices he has found at last his "garden of the Lord."

There are families from Jolland, from Killingworth and
    Lyme;
Gentle mothers, tender maidens, and strong men in their
    prime;
There are lovers who have plighted their vows in
    Coventry,
And merry children, dancing o'er the vessels' decks in
    glee.

They come as came the Hebrews into their promised
    land,
Not as to wild New England's shores came first the
    Pilgrim band,
The Minas fields were fruitful, and the Gaspereau had
    borne
To seaward many a vessel with its freight of yellow corn.

They come with hearts as true as their manners blunt and
    cold,
To found a race of noble men of stern New England
    mould,
A race of earnest people, whom the coming years shall
    teach
The broader ways of knowledge and the gentler forms of
    speech.

They come as Puritans, but who shall say their hearts are
    blind
To the subtle charms of Nature and the love of human-
    kind!
The Blue Laws of Connecticut have shaped their thought,
    'tis true,
But human laws can never wholly Heaven's work undo.

And tears fall fast from many an eye long time unused to
    weep,
For o'er the fields lay whitening the bones of cows and
    sheep—
The faithful cows that used to feed upon the broad Grand
    Pré,
And with their tinkling bells come slowly home at close
    of day.

And where the Acadian village stood, its roofs o'ergrown
    with moss,
And the simple wooden chapel with its altar and its cross,
And where the forge of Basil sent its sparks towards the
    sky,
The lonely thistle blossomed and the fire-weed grew high.

    .   .   .   .

The broken dykes have been rebuilt a century and more,
The cornfields stretch their furrows from Canard to Beauséjour,
Five generations have been reared beside the fair Grand Pré
Since the vessels from Connecticut came sailing up the Bay.

And now across the meadows, while the farmers reap and sow,
The engine shrieks its discords to the hills of Gaspereau;
And ever onward to the sea, the restless Fundy tide
Bears playful pleasure-yachts and busy trade ships side by side.

And the Puritan has yielded to the softening touch of time,
Like him who still content remained in Killingworth and Lyme;
And graceful homes of prosperous men make all the landscape fair,
And mellow creeds and ways of life are rooted everywhere.

And churches nestle lovingly on many a glad hillside,
And holy bells ring out their music in the eventide;
But here and there, on untilled ground, apart from glebe or town,
Some lone surviving apple tree stands leafless, bare and brown.

And many a traveller has found, as thoughtlessly he strayed,
Some long-forgotten cellar in the deepest thicket's shade,
And clumps of willows by the dykes, sweet-scented, fair and green,
That seemed to tell again the story of Evangeline.

AT THE CEDARS.

Duncan Campbell Scott.

You had two girls, Baptiste,
    One is Virginie ——
Hold hard, Baptiste,
    Listen to me.

The whole drive was jammed,
In that bend at the Cedars;
The rapids were dammed,
With the logs tight rammed
And crammed; you might know
The devil had clinched them below.

We worked three days—not a budge!
"She's as tight as a wedge,
On the ledge."
Says our foreman,
"Mon Dieu! boys, look here,
We must get this thing clear."
He cursed at the men,
And we went for it then,

With our cant-dogs arow;
We just gave "he yo ho,"
When she gave a big shove
From above.

The gang yelled, and tore
For the shore;
The logs gave a grind,
Like a wolf's jaws behind,
And as quick as a flash,
With a shove and a crash,
They were down in a mash.
But I, and ten more,
All, but Isaàc Dufour,
Were ashore.

He leaped on a log in front of the rush,
And shot out from the bind,
While the jam roared behind;
As he floated along,
He balanced his pole,
And tossed us a song.

But, just as we cheered,
Up darted a log from the bottom,
Leaped thirty feet, fair and square,
And came down on his own.

He went up like a block,
With the shock;
And when he was there,
In the air,

Kissed his hand
To the land.
When he dropped,
My heart stopped,
For the first logs had caught him,
And crushed him;
When he rose in his place
There was blood on his face.

There were some girls, Baptiste,
Picking berries on the hillside,
Where the river curls, Baptiste,
You know,—on the still side;
One was down by the water,
She saw Isaàc
Fall back.

She didn't scream, Baptiste;
She launched her canoe,—
It did seem, Baptiste,
That she wanted to die too,
For before you could think,
The birch cracked like a shell
In that rush of hell,
And I saw them both sink——

Baptiste!!——

He had two girls,
One is Virginie;
What God calls the other,
Is not known to me.

ROSE LATULIPPE.

(A French-Canadian Legend.)

"SERANUS."

The story or ballad of Ma'amselle Rose,
Surnamed Latulippe, as the story goes.

Seventeen hundred and forty, I'm told,
The winter was long and dark and cold.

The frosts were hard, and the snows were deep,
Lake and river were wrapped in sleep.

The days so short, and the food so dear,
At Christmas-time made sorry cheer.

The drifts piled high, and the roads left bare,
Made New Year's Day a slow affair.

Yet Nöel and New Year's as Paradise were
To Lent with its vision of fasting and prayer.

And lively girls like Ma'amselle Rose,
In her dark-blue skirt and her scarlet hose,

All over the country felt the same,
With their restless feet and their eyes of flame,

Striving to make the most of their fun
Ere Mardi-Gras should behold it done.

The day before has Ma'amselle Rose,
Standing on tip of her little toes,

Petitioned her father with modest glance
To let her give—a little dance.

And here we know just what came about,
For Rose, too cunning to beg or pout,

At once is accorded—so frank, so sweet,
Who could refuse her?—the wished-for treat.

Great were the preparations then,
The asking of girls, the finding of men;

For partners are rare in this wild new land,
Where girls grow as ripe and ready to hand

As in any tropical island or town
(Lying becalmed 'neath a starry crown,

Rich with clustering fruit and flower,
With gaudy creeper and glowing bower),

Though few are as fair as Ma'amselle Rose,
In her dark-blue skirt and her scarlet hose.

As for Mardi-Gras—*ciel!* What a day,
The wind it blew this way, that way,—

All ways at once, you would have said,
Till the snow was whirled far over the head,

And towards the evening a storm uprose
Which frightened all save Ma'amselle Rose.

The windows rattled—what did she care?
She was upstairs plaiting her long brown hair.

The watch-dog howled, but she did not hear,
She was hanging an earring in either ear;

And, thinking of onyx and filigree,
And musing, of these, which shall it be,

She hardly observes old Mère Marmette,
Who has come in a tremble to look for her pet.

Old Mère Marmette, with her withered face,
Under the cap with its starched white lace,

Just as one sees, in a cold March wood,
An old brown leaf with its snowy hood

Pushed back a little, that one may know
Will melt full soon the frost and the snow.

"O Rose, *chèrie*, did you not hear me call?
I fear for you, child, and I fear for us all!

'Tis the wildest night the Curé has known,
And to hear that good dog howl and moan

Is enough to drive one on to one's knees,
Though there, to be sure, we all might freeze

Such a night as this!" "Why, how you talk!"
Says Ma'amselle Rose, as she stops in her walk

To drape her flowered Indian shawl,
Thinking it makes her look quite tall.

"*Mon Dieu!* you talk," says Ma'amselle Rose,
With her laughing eye and her petulant pose,

"As if we had not seen nights as dark,
Or had never heard old Pierrot bark!"

Then to the window quick she flies—
"Look, Mère Marmette, look, look, what eyes!

What a figure! what grace! what a noble steed!
Now, who can it be? Now who, indeed?"

"*Ciel!* I know not! Some stranger bold—
The town is full of such, I'm told;

And Rose Latulippe, look you, do not forget
The last advice of your old Marmette,

Dance, dance, little Rose, dance all you like
Till the midnight hour from the clock shall strike;

But to dance after twelve to-night is a *sin*,
Whether with stranger or kith or kin.

And the Curé says——" "I know, I know,
Good mother Marmette, you tease one so!"

And with in the mirror a flying peep,
Away to the dance flies Rose Latulippe.

Already the guests are gathering all
In the long low room and the narrow hall,

Where hang the rude sticks and the stout raquettes,
And the great fur coats in patches wet

With the falling snow, that still outside
Is whirled aloft in an eddying tide!

There are the tenants from west and east,
From north to south, all bidden to feast

On pâtés, and fowls, and ragoûts immense,
All at their generous Seigneur's expense.

And here is old Jacques, the blind habitant,
Who can sing you the whole of *Le Juif Errant*,

And play on his fiddle such tunes so gay,
As *Le vent frivolant*, and *J'ai tant dansé*.

And now all the Seigneury forms in a line,
Then the *Grande Proménade* with an air so fine,

One can hardly believe it is "homespun grey"
And "*bottes sauvages*" who are leading the way.

And next they engage in a merry round dance,
Imported, of course, direct from France,

Which must surely gladden our gay little Rose,
In her dark-blue skirt and her scarlet hose.

But where is Rose? In the window seat
She seems to have found a cosy retreat,

And with her the stranger, tall and bold,
From her window she saw alight in the cold.

His eyes flash fire, and his brow is stern,
Yet his words with a thrilling music burn.

He knows her name, he has called her Rose,
Till her cheek with a brighter crimson glows;

He takes her hand, he holds it fast,
And into the circle they slip at last.

Then who so happy as little Rose,
While her red cheek redder and redder grows!

Again and again they dance like this,
And once has the stranger stolen a kiss,

That has almost frightened our brave little Rose—
Like a shudder of fire through her frame it goes—

Till the girls all stand in a whispering ring,
And deem it the very strangest thing,

That Rose should have known this cavalier,
And finish by deeming it *very queer*,—

As girls in all ages somehow do
When they have not been courted too.

But Mère Marmette is troubled still,
She follows her pet about until

The stranger has thrown her a wicked glance
That might have sent her into a trance,

Had she not quickly crossed herself,
And gone on washing and drying the delf;

For now, the feasting and supper all done,
Is the very height of Mardi-Gras fun.

Soon it will be the midnight hour
When to dance or play will be out of the power

Of all good Catholics, young and old,
Who wish to remain in the Church's fold.

But so proud and happy is Ma'amselle Rose,
In her dark-blue skirt and her scarlet hose,

With the stranger's arm around her waist,
And her hand on his shoulder lightly placed,

That when he beseeches for one turn more,
She slips on his arm out through the door

Into the dim and narrow hall,
Where creep the long shadows up the wall.

And lo, in a minute or less, that same Rose,
Surnamed Latulippe, as the story goes,

In the stranger's arms is spinning around
To a strange and diabolical sound,

Which cometh from no known instrument,
As old blind Jacques, in his corner intent

On a big pork pâté, very well knows :
Alas for poor little Ma'amselle Rose !

For presently, louder than Rose quite likes,
The tall old clock on the staircase strikes.

"*Mon Dieu !*" she cries, "you must let me go ;
'Tis twelve and after !"   "Nay, nay, not so !

I have you, and hold you, and fold you tight,
You are mine," says the stranger, "from to-night.

Dance, dance, little Rose, a word in your ear,
You are dancing with Lucifer, what dost thou fear ?"

.   .   .   .   .   .

The Curé ! the Curé !   He takes it all in,
From Rose, in her peril of horrible sin,

To Mother Marmette and the agèd Seigneur,
The whispering girls and the dazed voyageur.

And breathing a hurried and silent prayer,
And making the sign of the cross in the air,

And saying aloud, "The Church hath power
To save her children in such an hour,"

He taketh the maiden by both her hands,
Whilst Lucifer dark and discomfited stands ;

Snorting and stamping in fiendish ire,
He gains his steed with the eyes of fire,

Who gives one loud and terrible neigh,
And then in the darkness thunders away.

. . . . . .

ADIEU TO FRANCE.

(From "De Roberval.")

JOHN HUNTER-DUVAR.

Adieu to France! my latest glance
    Falls on thy port and bay, Rochelle;
The sunrays on the surf-curls dance,
    And springtime, like a pleasing spell,
Harmonious holds the land and sea.
    How long, alas, I cannot tell,
Ere this scene will come back to me!

The hours fleet fast, and on the mast
    Soon shall I hoist the parting sail;
Soon will the outer bay be passed,
    And on the skyline eyes will fail
To see a streak that means the land.
    On, then! before the tides and gale,
Hope at the helm, and in God's hand.

What doom I meet, my heart will beat
    For France, the débonnaire and gay;
She ever will in memory's seat
    Be present to my mind alway.
Hope whispers my return to you,
    Dear land, but should Fate say me nay,
And this should be my latest view,
    Fair France, loved France, *my* France, adieu!
Salut à la France, salut!

V.—SETTLEMENT LIFE.

V.—SETTLEMENT LIFE.

SONG OF THE AXE.

Isabella Valancey Crawford.

High grew the snow beneath the low-hung sky,
And all was silent in the wilderness;
In trance of stillness Nature heard her God
Rebuilding her spent fires, and veil'd her face
While the Great Worker brooded o'er His work.

"Bite deep and wide, O Axe, the tree,
What doth thy bold voice promise me?"

"I promise thee all joyous things,
That furnish forth the lives of kings!

"For ev'ry silver ringing blow,
Cities and palaces shall grow!"

"Bite deep and wide, O Axe, the tree,
Tell wider prophecies to me."

"When rust hath gnaw'd me deep and red,
A nation strong shall lift his head!

"His crown the very Heav'ns shall smite,
Æons shall build him in his might!"

"Bite deep and wide, O Axe, the tree;
Bright Seer, help on thy prophecy!"

Max smote the snow-weigh'd tree, and lightly laugh'd.
"See, friend," he cried to one that look'd and smil'd,
"My axe and I—we do immortal tasks—
We build up nations—this my axe and I!"

FIRE IN THE WOODS; OR, THE OLD SETTLER'S STORY.

Alexander M'Lachlan.

When first I settled in the woods,
    There were no neighbours nigh,
And scarce a living thing, save wolves,
    And Molly dear, and I.
We had our troubles, ne'er a doubt,
    In those wild woods alone;
But then, sir, I was bound to have
    A homestead of my own.

This was my field of battle, and
    The forest was my foe,
And here I fought with ne'er a thought,
    Save "lay the giants low."
I toiled in hope—got in a crop,
    And Molly watched the cattle;
To keep those "breachy" steers away,
    She had a weary battle.

The devil's dears were those two steers,—
    Ah, they were born fence-breakers!
And sneaked all day, and watched their prey,
    Like any salt-sea wreckers.
And gradually, as day by day,
    My crop grew golden yellow,
My heart and hope grew with that crop,—
    I was a happy fellow.

That crop would set me on my feet,
    And I'd have done with care;
I built away, the live-long day,
    Such "castles in the air!"
I'd beaten poverty at last,
    And, like a little boy
When he has got his first new coat,
    I fairly leapt for joy.

I blush to think upon it yet
    That I was such a fool;
But young folks must learn wisdom, sir,
    In old Misfortune's school.

One fatal night, I thought the wind
   Gave some unwonted sighs,
Down through the swamp I heard a tramp
   Which took me by surprise.

Is this an earthquake drawing near?
   The forest moans and shivers;
And then I thought that I could hear
   The rushing of great rivers;
And while I looked and listened there,
   A herd of deer swept by,
As from a close pursuing foe
   They madly seem'd to fly.

But still those sounds, in long deep bounds,
   Like warning heralds came,
And then I saw, with fear and awe,
   The heavens were all aflame.
I knew the woods must be on fire,
   I trembled for my crop;
As I stood there, in mute despair,
   It seem'd the death of hope.

On, on it came, a sea of flame,
   In long deep rolls of thunder,
And drawing near, it seem'd to tear
   The heavens and earth asunder!
How those waves snored, and raged, and roared,
   And reared in wild commotion!
On, on they came, like steeds of flame
   Upon a burning ocean.

How they did snort, in fiendish sport,
    As at the great elms dashing;
And how they tore 'mong hemlocks hoar,
    And through the pines went crashing;
While serpents wound the trunks around,
    Their eyes like demons gleaming.
And wrapped like thongs around the prongs,
    And to the crests went screaming!

Ah! how they swept, and madly leapt,
    From shrinking spire to spire,
'Mid hissing hail, and in their trail
    A waving lake of fire!
Anon some whirlwind, all aflame,
    Growled in the ocean under;
Then up would reel a fiery wheel
    And belch forth smoke and thunder!

And it was all that we could do
    To save ourselves by flight,
As from its track we madly flew,—
    Oh! 'twas an awful night!
When all was past, I stood aghast,
    My crop and shanty gone,
And blackened trunks 'mid smouldering chunks
    Like spectres looking on!

A host of skeletons they seemed,
    Amid the twilight dim,
All standing there in their despair,
    With faces gaunt and grim;

And I stood like a spectre too,
   A ruined man was I,
And nothing left,—what could I do
   But sit me down and cry?

A heavy heart indeed was mine,
   For I was ruined wholly,
And I gave way that awful day
   To moping melancholy;
I lost my all, in field and stall,
   And nevermore would thrive,
All save those steers,—the devil's dears
   Had saved themselves alive.

Nor would I have a farm to-day,
   Had it not been for Molly,
She cheered me up, and charmed away
   My moping melancholy;
She schemed and planned to keep the land,
   And cultivate it too,
And how I moiled, and strained, and toiled,
   And fought the battle through.

Yes, Molly played her part full well;
   She's plucky, every inch, sir!
It seemed to me the "deil himsel'"
   Could not make Molly flinch, sir;
We wrought and fought, until our star
   Got into the ascendant;
At troubles past we smile at last,
   And now we're independent!

BURNT LANDS.

Charles G. D. Roberts.

On other fields and other scenes the morn
    Laughs from her blue,—but not such scenes are these,
    Where comes no summer cheer of leaves and bees,
And no shade mitigates the day's white scorn.
These serious acres vast no groves adorn;
    But giant trunks, bleak shapes that once were trees,
    Tower naked, unassuaged of rain or breeze,
Their stern grey isolation grimly borne.

The months roll over them, and mark no change;
    But when spring stirs, or autumn stills, the years,
        Surely some phantom leafage rustles faint
Thro' their parched dreams,—some old-time notes ring strange,
    When in his slender treble, far and clear,
    Reiterates the rain-bird his complaint.

From "MALCOLM'S KATIE."

Isabella Valancey Crawford.

The South Wind laid his moccasins aside,
Broke his gay calumet of flow'rs, and cast
His useless wampun, beaded with cool dews,
Far from him, northward; his long ruddy spear

Flung sunward, whence it came; and his soft locks
Of warm fine haze grew silver as the birch.
His wigwam of green leaves began to shake;
The crackling rice-beds scolded harsh like squaws;
The small ponds pouted up their silver lips;
The great lakes ey'd the mountains,—whisper'd "Ugh!
Are ye so tall, O chiefs?"   "Not taller than
Our plumes can reach,"—and rose a little way,
As panthers stretch to try their velvet limbs,
And then retreat to purr and bide their time.
At morn the sharp breath of the night arose
From the wide prairies, in deep-struggling seas,
In rolling breakers, bursting to the sky;
In tumbling surfs, all yellow'd faintly thro'
With the low sun; in mad, conflicting crests,
Voic'd with low thunder from the hairy throats
Of the mist-buried herds; and for a man
To stand amid the cloudy roll and moil,
The phantom waters breaking overhead,
Shades of vex'd billows bursting on his breast,
Torn caves of mist wall'd with a sudden gold,
Reseal'd as swift as seen,—broad, shaggy fronts,
Fire-ey'd and tossing on impatient horns
The wave impalpable,—was but to think
A dream of phantoms held him as he stood!
The late, last thunders of the summer crash'd
Where shriek'd great eagles, lords of naked cliffs;
The pulseless Forest, lock'd and interlock'd
So closely, bough with bough, and leaf with leaf,
So serf'd by its own wealth, that while from high
The moons of summer kiss'd its green-gloss'd locks,
And round its knees the merry West Wind danc'd,
And round its ring-compacted emerald,
The South Wind crept on moccasins of flame,
And the red fingers of th' impatient Sun

Pluck'd at its outmost fringes,—its dim veins
Beat with no life; its deep and dusky heart,
In a deep trance of shadow, felt no throb
To such soft wooing answer! Thro' its dream
Brown rivers of deep waters sunless stole;
Small creeks sprang from its mosses, and amaz'd,
Like children in a wigwam curtain'd close
Above the great dead heart of some red chief,
Slipp'd on soft feet, swift stealing through the gloom,
Eager for light and for the frolic winds.
In this shrill Moon the scouts of winter ran
From the ice-belted north, and whistling shafts
Struck maple and struck sumach, and a blaze
Ran swift from leaf to leaf, from bough to bough;
Till round the forest flash'd a belt of flame,
And inward lick'd its tongues of red and gold
To the deep tranced inmost heart of all.
Rous'd the still heart,—but all too late, too late!
Too late the branches, welded fast with leaves,
Toss'd, loosen'd to the winds; too late the Sun
Pour'd his last vigour to the deep dark cells
Of the dim wood! The keen two-bladed Moon
Of Falling Leaves roll'd up on crested mists;
And where the lush rank boughs had foiled the Sun
In his red prime, her pale sharp fingers crept
After the wind, and felt about the moss,
And seem'd to pluck from shrinking twig and stem
The burning leaves,—while groaned the shudd'ring
    wood!

  .   .   .   .

The mighty morn strode laughing up the land,
And Max, the labourer and the lover, stood
Within the forest's edge, beside a tree,—
The mossy king of all the woody tribes,—

Whose clatt'ring branches rattl'd, shuddering,
As the bright axe cleav'd moon-like thro' the air,
Waking strange thunders, rousing echoes link'd
From the full lion-throated roar to sighs
Stealing on dove-wings thro' the distant aisles.
Swift fell the axe, swift follow'd roar on roar,
Till the bare woodland bellow'd in its rage
As the first-slain slow toppl'd to his fall.
"O King of Desolation, art thou dead?"
Thought Max, and laughing, heart and lips, leap'd on
The vast prone trunk.   "And have I slain a King?
Above his ashes will I build my house;—
No slave beneath its pillars, but—a King!"

  . . . . . .

It was not all his own, the axe-stirr'd waste.
In these new days men spread about the earth,
With wings at heel,—and now the settler hears,
While yet his axe rings on the primal woods,
The shrieks of engines rushing o'er the wastes,
Nor parts his kind to hew his fortunes out.
And as one drop glides down the unknown rock,
And the bright-threaded stream leaps after it
With welded billions, so the settler finds
His solitary footsteps beaten out
With the quick rush of panting human waves,
Upheav'd by throbs of angry poverty,
And driven by keen blasts of hunger, from
Their native strands,—so stern, so dark, so drear!
O, then, to see the troubl'd, groaning waves,
Throb down to peace in kindly valley beds,
Their turbid bosoms clearing in the calm
Of sun-ey'd Plenty,—till the stars and moon,
The blessed sun himself, has leave to shine
And laugh in their dark hearts! So shanties grew

Other than his amid the blacken'd stumps;
And children ran with little twigs and leaves,
And flung them, shouting, on the forest pyres,
Where burn'd the forest kings,—and in the glow
Paus'd men and women when the day was done.
There the lean weaver ground anew his axe,
Nor backward look'd upon the vanish'd loom,
But forward, to the ploughing of his fields,
And to the rose of Plenty in the cheeks
Of wife and children, nor heeded much the pangs
Of the rous'd muscles tuning to new work;
The pallid clerk look'd on his blister'd palms,
And sigh'd and smil'd, but girded up his loins,
And found new vigour as he felt new hope;
The lab'rer, with train'd muscles, grim and grave,
Look'd at the ground, and wonder'd in his soul
What joyous anguish stirr'd his darken'd heart
At the mere look of the familiar soil,
And found his answer in the words—"*Mine own!*"
Then came smooth-coated men, with eager eyes,
And talk'd of steamers on the cliff-bound lakes,
And iron tracks across the prairie lands,
And mills to crush the quartz of wealthy hills,
And mills to saw the great wide-armèd trees,
And mills to grind the singing stream of grain;
And with such busy clamour mingled still
The throbbing music of the bold, bright Axe,—
The steel tongue of the Present, and the wail
Of falling forest,—voices of the Past.

 Max, social-soul'd, and with his practised thews,
Was happy, boy-like, thinking much of Kate,
And speaking of her to the women-folk;
Who, mostly, happy in new honeymoons
Of hope themselves, were ready still to hear
The thrice-told tale of Katie's sunny eyes,

And Katie's yellow hair, and household ways;
And heard so often, "There shall stand our home,
On yonder slope, with vines about the door!"
That the good wives were almost made to see
The snowy walls, deep porches, and the gleam
Of Katie's garments flitting through the rooms.—
And the black slope, all bristling with burn'd stumps,
Was known amongst them all as "Max's House."

  O Love builds on the azure sea,
   And Love builds on the golden sand;
  And Love builds on the rose-wing'd cloud,
   And sometimes Love builds on the land.

  Or if Love builds on sparkling sea,
   And if Love builds on golden strand,
  And if Love builds on rosy cloud,—
   To Love, these are the solid land.

  O Love will build his lily walls,
   And Love his pearly roof will rear,
  On cloud or land, or mist or sea,—
   Love's solid land is everywhere!

THE SECOND CONCESSION OF DEER.

William Wye Smith.

John Tompkins lived in a house of logs,
   On the second concession of Deer;
The front was logs, all straight and sound—
The gable was logs, all tight and round—
The roof was logs, so firmly bound—
And the floor was logs, all down to the ground—
      The warmest house in Deer.

And John, to my mind, was a log himself,
   On the second concession of Deer;—
None of your birch, with bark of buff—
Nor basswood, weak and watery stuff—
But he was hickory, true and tough,
And only his outside bark was rough;—
      The grandest old man in Deer!

But John had lived too long, it seemed,
   On the second concession of Deer!
For his daughters up the governing rein,
With a fine brick house on the old domain,
All papered, and painted with satinwood stain,
Carpeted stairs, and best ingrain—
      The finest house in Deer!

Poor John, it was sad to see him now,
   On the second concession of Deer!
When he came in from his weary work,

To strip off his shoes like a heathen Turk,—
Or out of the *company's* way to lurk,
And ply in the *shanty* his knife and fork—
      The times were turned in Deer!

But John was hickory to the last,
   On the second concession of Deer!
And out on the river-end of his lot,
He laid up the logs in a cosy spot,
And self and wife took up with a cot,
And the great brick house might swim or not—
      He was done with the pride of Deer!

But the great house could not go at all,
   On the second concession of Deer;
'Twas *mother* no more, to wash or bake,
Nor *father* the gallants' steeds to take—
From the kitchen no more came pie nor cake—
And even their butter they'd first to make!—
      There were lessons to learn in Deer!

And the lesson they learned a year or more,
   On the second concession of Deer!
Then the girls got back the brave old pair—
And gave the mother her easy-chair—
She told them how, and they did their share—
And John the honours once more did wear
      Of his own domain in Deer!

A CANADIAN FOLK-SONG.

William Wilfred Campbell.

The doors are shut, the windows fast,
Outside the gust is driving past,
Outside the shivering ivy clings,
While on the hob the kettle sings,—
Margery, Margery, make the tea,
Singeth the kettle merrily.

The streams are hushed up where they flowed,
The ponds are frozen along the road,
The cattle are housed in shed and byre,
While singeth the kettle on the fire;
Margery, Margery, make the tea,
Singeth the kettle merrily.

The fisherman on the bay in his boat
Shivers and buttons up his coat;
The traveller stops at the tavern door,
And the kettle answers the chimney's roar,—
Margery, Margery, make the tea,
Singeth the kettle merrily.

The firelight dances upon the wall,
Footsteps are heard in the outer hall,
And a kiss and a welcome that fill the room,
And the kettle sings in the glimmer and gloom,—
Margery, Margery, make the tea,
Singeth the kettle merrily.

"THE INJUN."

(An Incident in the Minnesota Massacre of 1862.)

John E. Logan—"Barry Dane."

Ye say the Injuns all alike,
  A bad an' sneakin' lot;
An' a'int no use for nuthin',
  So the cusses should be shot?

Well, p'raps they is, an' p'raps they a'int,
  A lazy, wuthless crowd;
Yet durn my skin ef I kin see
  Why white men chin so loud.

Ef some o' them poor devils kicks
  'Cause things a'int run quite squar',
An' jumps an Indian agent's ranch,
  An' yanks his bloomin' har,

'Thar' a'int no thought uv causes,
  An' no one cares a cuss,
It's jes' call out the Blue Coats
  An' give 'em somethin' wuss.

Thar's good an' bad in Injun,
  An' thar's good an' bad in White;
But, somehow, they is allus wrong,
  An' we is allus right.

But I'm an old, old timer,
   I've jes' bin here so long,
That I kin mostly allus tell
   The ones that's right an' wrong.

An' ye can bet yer sainted life,
   When things get steamin' hot,
That some white fool or knave has lit
   The fire that biles the pot.

Ye think the Injun isn't squar'?
   That's jes' whar' ye mistake;
Fer bein' true to them that's true
   The Injun scoops the cake.

Fer I kin tell ye what occurr'd
   Way back in 'sixty-two,
When things in Minnesota State
   Wuz lookin' kinder blue.

The Sioux wuz up an' on the shoot,
   A-slingin' round their lead,
An' scalpin' every mother's son
   That wuzn't bald or dead.

Thar' warn't a livin' Yankee—
   An' lots wuz brave an' bold—
That would have crossed them plains alone
   For a waggon load uv gold.

'Cause why? We know'd the Guv'ment
   Wuzn't treatin' Injuns fair;
That's why they riz an' painted things,
   An' raised the settlers' hair.

That summer a fur-trader
   Come up from Montreal,
An' on his way to Garry
   He landed at Saint Paul.

An' all the guides an' hunters said
   He couldn't cross the plains,
Fer them thar' painted devils
   Wuz layin' low fer trains.

He only laffed, and said, he know'd
   The Injuns all his life,
An' he wuz goin' to mosey through
   An' take along his wife.

An' she, you bet, wuz plucky,
   An' said she'd go along,
Fer Injuns only went fer them
   As allus done 'em wrong.

Now I should smile, 'twuz riskey—
   An' all the fellers sed
The chances of their gettin' through,
   Warn't wuth an ounce uv lead.

But sure's yer born they started,
   Right out the northern trail,
Aboard a praree schooner,
   With a Texan steer fer sail.

An' right a-top that creekin' cart,
   Upon the highest rack,
That trader nailed a bloomin' rag—
   An English Union Jack.

So thar' he'd gone an' done it,
   Es stubborn as a mule;
An' knowin' fellers said we'd seen
   The last of that damn fool.

They wuzn't long upon the trail,
   Before a band of Reds
Got on their tracks, an' foller'd up,
   A-goin' to shave their heads.

But when they seen that little flag
   A-stickin' on that cart,
They jes' said, "Hudson Bay. Go on.
   Good trader with good heart!"

An' when they struck the river,
   An' took to their canoe,
'Twuz that thar' bit uv culler
   That seen 'em safely through.

Fer thar' that cussed little rag
    Went floatin' through the State—
A-flappin' in the face uv death,
    An' smilin' right at fate.

That wuz the way them 'tarnal fools
    Crossed them thar' blazin' plains,
An' floated down the windin' Red
    Through waves with bloody stains.

What give that flag its virtoo?
    What's thar' in red an' blue,
To make a man an' woman dar'
    What others deasn't do?

Jes' this—an' Injuns know'd it—
    That whar' them cullers flew,
The men that lived beneath them
    Wuz mostly straight an' true.

That when they made a bargain,
    'Twuz jes' as strong an' tight
As if 't were drawn on sheep-skin
    An' signed in black an' white.

That's how them Hudson traders done
    Fer mor'n two hundred year;
That's why that trader feller crossed
    Them plains without a fear.

An' jes' so long es white men
    Don't try some little game,
To euchre out the red man,
    So long he'll act the same.

But when the men beneath that flag,
    Tries any monkey ways,
Then, good-bye, old time friendship,
    For the Injuns goin' ter raise.

But jes' believe me, onst for all,
    To them that treats him fair,
The Injun mostly allus wuz,
    And is, and will be, square.

VI.—SPORTS AND FREE LIFE.

VI.—SPORTS AND FREE LIFE.

THE WRAITH OF THE RED SWAN.*

BLISS CARMAN.

WHY tarries the flash of his blade?
  At morning he sailed from me;
From the depth of our high beech glade,
  To the surge and the sea
I followed the gleam of his blade.

The cherries were flowering white,
  And the Nashwaak Islands flooded,
When the long Red Swan took flight;
  On a wind she scudded
With her gunwale buried from sight,
Till her sail drew down out of sight.

* "The Red Swan" is the author's favourite birch bark canoe, so named by him from the phenomenal rosiness of its bark material.

He shouted, "A northward track,
    Before the swallows have flown!"
And now the cherries are black,
    And the clover is brown,
And the Red Swan comes not back.

The stream-bends, hidden and shy,
    With their harvest of lilies are strewn;
The gravel bars are all dry,
    And warm in the noon,
Where the rapids go swirling by,—
Go singing and rippling by.

Through many an evening gone,
    Where the roses drank the breeze,
When the pale slow moon outshone
    Through the slanting trees,
I dreamed of the long Red Swan.

How I should know that one
    Great stroke, and the time of the swing
Urging her on and on,
    Spring after spring,
Lifting the long Red Swan,
Lifting the long Red Swan!

How I should drink the foam—
    The far white lines from her swift
Keen bow, when, hurrying to come,
    With lift upon lift
The long Red Swan came home!

Here would I crouch down low,
    And watch the Red Swan from far,
A speck in the evening, grow
      To a flaming star
In the dusk as of ages ago,
In the dusk of ages ago.

I would lean, and with lips apart,
    See the streak of the Red Swan's fire
Glow dim at the twilight's heart,—
      Feel the core of desire
From the slumber of years upstart.

How soon should the day grow wan,
    And a wind from the south unfold,
Like the low beginning of dawn,—
      Grow steady and hold
In the race of the long Red Swan,
In the race of the long Red Swan!

How glad of their river once more
    Would the crimson wings unfurl,
And the long Red Swan, on the roar
      Of a whitecap swirl,
Steer in to the arms of her shore!

But the wind is the voice of a dirge!
    What wonder allures him, what care,
So far on the world's bleak verge?
      Why lingers he there,
By the sea and the desolate surge,
In the sound of the moan of the surge?

Last midnight the thunder rode
　　With the lightning astride of the storm
Low down in the east, where glowed
　　The fright of his form
On the ocean-wild rack he bestrode.

The hills were his ocean wan,
　　And the white tree tops foamed high,
Lashed out of the night, whereon
　　In a gust fled by
A wraith of the long Red Swan,
A wraith of the long Red Swan.

Her crimson bellying sail
　　Was fleckered with brine and spume;
Its taut wet clew, through the veil
　　Of the driving fume,
Was sheeted home on the gale.

The shoal of the fury of night
　　Was a bank in the fog, wherethrough
Hissed the Red Swan in her flight;
　　She shrilled as she flew,
A shriek from the seething white,
In the face of the world grown white.

She laboured not in the sea,
　　Careened but a handbreadth over,
And, the gleam of her side laid free
　　For the drift to cover,
Sped on to the dark in her lee.

Through crests of the hoarse tide swing,
    Clove sheer the sweep of her bow;
There was loosed the ice-roaring of Spring
    From the jaws of her prow,—
Of the long Red Swan full wing,
The long Red Swan full wing.

Where the rake of her gunwale dipped
    As the spent black waves ran aft,
In a hand for helm there was gripped
    The sheen of a haft,
Which sang in the furrows it ripped.

Then I knew and was glad, for what foam
    Could the rush of her speed o'erwhelm
If Louis and his Whitehaulm
    Were steersman and helm,
When the long Red Swan drave home,
When the long Red Swan drave home?

Yet ever the sweeping mist
    Was a veil to his face from me,
Though yearning I well half wist
    What his look might be
From the carven bend of his wrist.

Then a break, and the cloud was gone,
    And there was his set keen face
Afire with smouldering dawn
    In the joy of her race,
In the flight of the long Red Swan,
In the flight of the long Red Swan!

Though drenched in the spray-drift hoar,
    As of old it was ruddy and warm
Through the black hair, grizzled and frore,
    Whipped out on the storm;
Then "Louis!" I launched on the roar.

O'er night and the brawl of the stream
    The hail of my cry flew on;
He turned, with a smile supreme,
    And the long Red Swan
Grew dim as the wraith of a dream,
As the blown white wraith of a dream

Look! Burnished and blue, what a sweep
    Of river outwinds in the sun;
What miles of shimmering deep,
    Where the hills grow one
With their shadow of summer and sleep!

I gaze from the cedar shade
    Day long, high over the beach,
And never a ripple is laid
    To the long blue reach,
Where faded the gleam of that blade,
The far gold flash of his blade.

I follow and dream and recall,
    Forget and remember and dream;
When the interval grass waves tall,
    I move in the gleam
Where his blade-beats glitter and fall.

Yet never my dream gets clear
  Of the whispering bodeful spell
The aspen shudders to hear,
  Yet hurries to tell,—
How the long Red Swan draws near,
How the long Red Swan draws near.

BIRCH AND PADDLE.

To Bliss Carman.

CHARLES G. D. ROBERTS.

FRIEND, those delights of ours
Under the sun and showers,—

Athrough the noonday blue
Sliding our light canoe,

Or floating, hushed, at eve,
When the dim pine-tops grieve!

What tonic days were they
Where shy streams dart and play,—

Where rivers brown and strong
As caribou bound along,

Break into angry parle
Where wildcat rapids snarl,

Subside, and like a snake
Wind to the quiet lake !

We've paddled furtively,
Where giant boughs hide the sky,—

Have stolen, and held our breath,
Thro' coverts still as death,—

Have left, with wing unstirred,
The brooding phœbe-bird,

And hardly caused a care
In the water-spider's lair.

For love of his clear pipe
We've flushed the zigzag snipe,—

Have chased in wilful mood
The wood-duck's flapping brood,—

Have spied the antlered moose
Cropping the young green spruce,

And watched him till betrayed
By the kingfisher's sharp tirade.

Quitting the bodeful shades,
We've run thro' sunnier glades,

And dropping craft and heed
Have bid our paddles speed.

Where the mad rapids chafe
We've shouted, steering safe,—

With sinew tense, nerve keen,
Shot thro' the roar, and seen,

With spirit wild as theirs,
The white waves leap like hares.

And then, with souls grown clear
In that sweet atmosphere,

With influences serene,
Our blood and brain washed clean,

We've idled down the breast
Of broadening tides at rest,

And marked the winds, the birds,
The bees, the far-off herds,

Into a drowsy tune
Transmute the afternoon.

So, Friend, with ears and eyes,
Which shy divinities

Have opened with their kiss,
We need no balm but this,—

A little space for dreams
On care-unsullied streams,—

'Mid task and toil, a space
To dream on Nature's face

THE NOR'-WEST COURIER.

"Barry Dane"—John E. Logan.

I.

Up, my dogs, merrily,
  The morn sun is shining,
    Our path is uncertain,
    And night's sombre curtain
May drop on us, verily,
  Ere time for reclining;
  So, up, without whining,
You rascals, instanter,
  Come into your places
  There, stretch out your traces,
And off, at a canter.

II.

Up, my dogs, cheerily,
 The noon sun is glowing,
  Fast and still faster,
  Come, follow your master;
Or to-night we may wearily,
Tired and drearily,
 Travel, not knowing
  What moment disaster
May sweep in the storm-blast,
And over each form cast
 A shroud in its blowing.

III.

On, my dogs, steadily,
 Though keen winds are shifting
 The snowflakes, and drifting
  Them straight in our faces;
Come, answer me readily,
Not wildly nor headily,
 Plunging and lifting
  Your feet, keep your paces;
For yet we shall weather
The blizzard together,
 Though evil our case is.

IV.

Sleep, my dogs, cosily,
 Coiled near the fire,
 That higher and higher
Sheds its light rosily
Out o'er the snow and sky;

    Sleep in the ruddy glow,
      Letting Keewaydin blow
  Fierce in his ire.
    Sleep, my dogs, soundly;
    For to-morrow we roundly
  Must buffet the foe.

THE HALL OF SHADOWS.

Alexander M'Lachlan.

The sun is up, and through the woods
  His golden rays are streaming;
The dismal swamp, and swale so damp,
  With faces bright are beaming.
And in the wind-fall, by the creek,
  We hear the partridge drumming;
And strange bright things, on airy wings,
  Are all around us humming.

The merry schoolboys, in the woods
  The chipmunk are pursuing;
And as he starts, with happy hearts
  They're after him hallooing.
The squirrel hears the urchins' cheers,—
  They never catch him lagging,—
And on the beech, beyond their reach,
  Hear how the fellow's bragging!

The redbird pauses in his song,—
  The face of man aye fearing,—
And flashes, like a flame, along
  The border of the clearing.
The humming-bird, above the flower,
  Is like a halo bending;
Or like the gleams we catch in dreams
  Of heavenly things descending.

And hear the bugle of the bee
  Among the tufted clover!
This day, like thee, I'll wander free,
  My little wild-wood rover!
Through groves of beech, and maple green,
  And pines of lofty stature;
By this lone creek, once more we'll seek
  The savage haunts of nature.

See there a noble troop of pines
  Have made a sudden sally,
And all, in straight, unbroken lines,
  Are rushing up the valley;
And round about the lonely spring
  They gather in a cluster,
Then off again, till on the plain,
  The great battalions muster.

And there the little evergreens
  Are clust'ring in the hollows,
And hazels green, with sumachs lean,
  Among the weeping willows;

Or sit in pride the creek beside,
  Or through the valley ramble;
Or up the height, in wild delight,
  Among the rocks they scramble.

And here a gorge, all reft and rent,
  With rocks in wild confusion,
As they were by the wood-gods sent
  To guard them from intrusion;
And gulfs, all yawning wild and wide,
  As if by earthquakes shattered;
And rocks that stand,—a grizzly band!—
  By time and tempest battered.

Some great pines, blasted in their pride,
  Above the gorge are bending;
And rock-elms, from the other side
  Their mighty arms extending.
And midway down the dark descent
  One fearful hemlock's clinging;
His headlong fall he would prevent,
  And grapnels out he's flinging.

One ash has ventured to the brink,
  And tremblingly looks over
That awful steep, where shadows sleep,
  And mists at noonday hover.
But further in the woods we go,
  Through birch and maple valleys,
And elms that stand, like patriarchs grand,
  In long dark leafy alleys.

Away, away! from blue-eyed day,
   The sunshine and the meadows;
We find our way, at noon of day,
   Within the Hall of Shadows.
How like a great cathedral vast!
   With creeping vines roofed over,
While shadows dim, with faces grim,
   Far in the distance hover.

Among the old cathedral aisles,
   And Gothic arches bending,
And ever in the sacred pales
   The twilight gloom descending.
And let me turn where'er I will,
   A step is aye pursuing;
And there's an eye upon me still
   That's watching all I'm doing.

And in the centre there's a pool,
   And by that pool is sitting
A shape of Fear, with shadows drear
   For ever round her flitting.
Why is her face so full of woe?
   So hopeless and dejected?
Sees she but there, in her despair,
   Nought but herself reflected?

Is it the gloom within my heart,
   Or lingering superstition,
Which draws me here three times a year
   To this weird apparition?
I cannot tell what it may be!
   I only know that seeing
That shape of Fear, draws me more near
   The secret soul of being.

CANADIAN HUNTER'S SONG.

Susanna (Strickland) Moodie.

The Northern Lights are flashing
  On the rapids' restless flow;
But o'er the wild waves dashing
  Swift darts the light canoe,
    The merry hunters come,—
      "What cheer? What cheer?"
      "We've slain the deer!"
    "Hurrah! you're welcome home!"

The blithesome horn is sounding,
  And the woodman's loud halloo;
And joyous steps are bounding
  To meet the birch canoe.
    "Hurrah! the hunters come!"
      And the woods ring out
      To their noisy shout,
    As they drag the dun deer home!

The hearth is brightly burning,
  The rustic board is spread;
To greet their sire returning
  The children leave their bed.
    With laugh and shout they come,
      That merry band,
      To grasp his hand
    And bid him welcome home!

THE FISHERMAN'S LIGHT.

(*A Song of the Backwoods.*)

Mrs. (Susanna Strickland) Moodie.

The air is still,—the night is dark,—
  No ripple breaks the dusky tide;
From isle to isle the fisher's bark,
  Like fairy meteor, seems to glide,—
Now lost in shade,—now flashing bright;
  On sleeping wave and forest tree,
We hail with joy the ruddy light,
Which far into the darksome night
  Shines red and cheerily.

With spear high poised, and steady hand,
  The centre of that fiery ray
Behold the skilful fisher stand,
  Prepared to strike the finny prey;
"Now, now!" the shaft has sped below,—
  Transfixed the shining prize we see;
On swiftly glides the birch canoe,
The woods send back the long halloo
  In echoes loud and cheerily!

Around yon bluff, whose pine crest hides
  The noisy rapids from our sight,
Another bark, another glides,—
  Red spirits of the murky night,—
The bosom of the silent stream
  With mimic stars is dotted free;
The tall woods lighten in the beam,
  Through darkness shining cheerily.

THE KINGFISHER.

Charles Lee Barnes.

When the summer's bright and tender sunbeams fill the land with splendour,
In his robes of blue and purple, and his crown of burnished green,
Lone the kingfisher sits dreaming, with his dark eyes brightly gleaming,
While he peers for chub and minnows in the water's limpid sheen.

And he haunts the river's edges, oozy flats, and rustling sedges,
Till he sees his prey beneath him in the waters clear and cool;
Then he quickly dashes nearer, and he breaks the polished mirror
That was floating on the surface of the creek or hidden pool.

Where the nodding reeds are growing, and the yellow lilies blowing,
In our little boat we slowly glide along the placid stream;
And we know he's coming after, by the music of his laughter,
And the flashing of his vesture in the sun's effulgent beam.

Well he knows the alder bushes, and the slender slimy
    rushes,
And the swamp, and pond, and lakelet, and the ice-cold
    crystal spring;
And the brooklet oft he follows through the meadows
    and the hollows,
Far within the shadowy woodland where the thrush and
    robin sing.

Oh, he well can flutter proudly, and he well can laugh so
    loudly,
For he lives within a castle where he never knows a
    care!
And his realm is on the water, and his wife a monarch's
    daughter;
And his title undisputed is on earth, or sea, or air!

THE CANOE.

Isabella Valancey Crawford.

My masters twain made me a bed
Of pine-boughs resinous, and cedar;
Of moss, a soft and gentle breeder
Of dreams of rest; and me they spread
With furry skins, and, laughing, said,—
"Now she shall lay her polish'd sides,
As queens do rest, or dainty brides,
Our slender lady of the tides!"

My masters twain their camp-soul lit,
Streamed incense from the hissing cones;
Large crimson flashes grew and whirl'd,
Thin golden nerves of sly light curl'd,
Round the dun camp, and rose faint zones
Half-way about each grim bole knit,
Like a shy child that would bedeck
With its soft clasp a Brave's red neck;
Yet sees the rough shield on his breast,
The awful plumes shake on his crest,
And fearful drops his timid face,
Nor dares complete the sweet embrace.

Into the hollow hearts of brakes
Yet warm from sides of does and stags,
Pass'd to the crisp dark river flags,
Sinuous, red as copper, snakes,—
Sharp-headed serpents, made of light,
Glided and hid themselves in night.

My masters twain the slaughter'd deer
Hung on fork'd boughs—with thongs of
    leather.
Bound were his stiff slim feet together,—
His eyes like dead stars cold and drear;
The wand'ring firelight drew near
And laid its wide palm, red and anxious,
On the sharp splendour of his branches;
On the white foam grown hard and sere
  On flank and shoulder,—
Death, hard as breast of granite boulder,—
    And under his lashes
Peer'd thro' his eyes at his life's grey ashes.

My masters twain sang songs that wove
(As they burnish'd hunting blade and rifle)
A golden thread with a cobweb trifle,—
Loud of the chase, and low of love.

"O Love! art thou a silver fish,
Shy of the line, and shy of gaffing?
Which we do follow, fierce, yet laughing,
Casting at thee the light-wing'd wish;
And at the last shall we bring thee up
From the crystal darkness under the cup
    Of lily folden,
    On broad leaves golden?

"O Love! art thou a silver deer?
Swift thy starr'd feet as wing of swallow,
While we with rushing arrows follow;
And at the last shall we draw near,
And over thy velvet neck cast thongs,
Woven of roses, of stars, of songs,—
    New chains all moulden
    Of rare gems olden?"

They hung the slaughter'd fish like swords
On saplings slender,—like scimitars
Bright, and ruddied from new-dead wars,
Blaz'd in the light,—the scaly hordes.

They pil'd up boughs beneath the trees,
Of cedar-web and green fir tassel;
Low did the pointed pine tops rustle,
The camp fire blush'd to the tender breeze.

The hounds laid dew-laps on the ground,
With needles of pine, sweet, soft, and rusty,—
Dream'd of the dead stag, stout and lusty;
A bat by the red flames wove its round.

The darkness built its wigwam walls
Close round the camp, and at its curtain
Press'd shapes, thin woven and uncertain,
As white locks of tall waterfalls.

CANOE SONG.

Isabella Valancey Crawford.

O LIGHT canoe! where dost thou glide?
Below thee gleams no silver'd tide,
But concave heaven's chiefest pride.

Above thee burns eve's rosy bar;
Below thee throbs her darling star;
Deep 'neath thy keel her round worlds are!

Above, below, O sweet surprise!
To gladden happy lover's eyes;
No earth, no wave,—all jewelled skies!

THE WALKER OF THE SNOW.

Charles Dawson Shanly.

Speed on, speed on, good Master!
  The camp lies far away;
We must cross the haunted valley
  Before the close of day.

How the snow-blight came upon me
  I will tell you as I go,—
The blight of the Shadow-hunter,
  Who walks the midnight snow.

To the cold December heaven
  Came the pale moon and the stars,
As the yellow sun was sinking
  Behind the purple bars.

The snow was deeply drifted
  Upon the ridges drear,
That lay for miles around me
  And the camp for which we steer.

'Twas silent on the hillside,
  And by the solemn wood
No sound of life or motion
  To break the solitude,

Save the wailing of the moose-bird
   With a plaintive note and low,
And the skating of the red leaf
   Upon the frozen snow.

And said I, "Though dark is falling,
   And far the camp must be,
Yet my heart it would be lightsome,
   If I had but company."

And then I sang and shouted,
   Keeping measure, as I sped,
To the harp-twang of the snow-shoe
   As it sprang beneath my tread;

Nor far into the valley
   Had I dipped upon my way,
When a dusky figure joined me,
   In a capuchon of grey,

Bending upon the snow-shoes,
   With a long and limber stride;
And I hailed the dusky stranger,
   As we travelled side by side.

But no token of communion
   Gave he by word or look,
And the fear-chill fell upon me
   At the crossing of the brook.

For I saw by the sickly moonlight,
　As I followed, bending low,
That the walking of the stranger
　Left no footmarks on the snow.

Then the fear-chill gathered o'er me,
　Like a shroud around me cast,
As I sank upon the snow-drift
　Where the Shadow-hunter passed.

And the otter-trappers found me,
　Before the break of day,
With my dark hair blanched and whitened
　As the snow in which I lay.

But they spoke not as they raised me;
　For they knew that in the night
I had seen the Shadow-hunter,
　And had withered in his blight.

Sancta Maria speed us!
　The sun is falling low,—
Before us lies the valley
　Of the Walker of the Snow!

THE RAPID.

Charles Sangster.

All peacefully gliding,
The waters dividing,
The indolent bátteau moved slowly along,
The rowers, light-hearted,
From sorrow long parted,
Beguiled the dull moments with laughter and song:
"Hurrah for the Rapid! that merrily, merrily
Gambols and leaps on its tortuous way;
Soon we will enter it, cheerily, cheerily,
Pleased with its freshness, and wet with its spray."

More swiftly careering,
The wild Rapid nearing,
They dash down the stream like a terrified steed;
The surges delight them,
No terrors affright them,
Their voices keep pace with their quickening speed:
"Hurrah for the Rapid! that merrily, merrily
Shivers its arrows against us in play;
Now we have entered it cheerily, cheerily,
Our spirits as light as its feathery spray."

Fast downward they're dashing,
Each fearless eye flashing,
Though danger awaits them on every side;
Yon rock—see it frowning!
They strike—they are drowning!

But downward they sped with the merciless tide :
   No voice cheers the Rapid, that angrily, angrily
   Shivers their bark in its maddening play ;
Gaily they entered it—heedlessly, recklessly,
   Mingling their lives with its treacherous spray !

THE WINTER SPIRIT.

(The Origin of the Ice Palace.)

HELEN FAIRBAIRN.

THE winter night was full of wind and storm,
   The Christian's festal season close at hand,
With frosty, glistening, snow-besprinkled form,
   The Winter Spirit roamed throughout the land.

Beneath, his flying footsteps froze the ground ;
   And with his garments' rustling fell the snow ;
His lightest touch made icicles abound ;
   His breath, as when the keenest north winds blow.

He paused above the river, dull and gray,
   Turbid and chafing with a restless pain,
And soon in icy quietness it lay,
   Bound, bank to bank, within his Arctic chain.

He roamed along the leafless mountain side,
   And wheresoe'er he found a solemn spruce,
Or stately fir, or hemlock rich and wide,
   He paused, and shook his gleaming garments loose.

And from their ample folds came softly down
   A cloud of snowflakes like a starry mist,
That gave each evergreen a spotless crown,
   For faithful keeping of its winter tryst.

Amid the storm-tossed pines his voice was heard,
   A wild soft sighing in their depths profound,
Like notes of some strange ghostly winter bird,
   Whose white wings fluttered with a muffled sound.

To lighter, more fantastic work, anon
   He turned, and, with a skill that art surpassed,
Drew strange designs and fairy forms upon
   The casements closed against the winter blast.

At one he longer paused than all the rest,
   And whispered in a frosty monotone,
"This work shall be my rarest and my best,
   Rarest and best is she for whom 'tis done."

He knew the girlish face with heavenly eyes,
   The fair sweet face whose eyes, so deep and blue,
Would kindle to their depths with glad surprise,
   At sight of what his frosty skill could do.

Without a sound the wintry work was done,
   With wondrous haste the icy picture grew,
And when at last the crowning point was won,
   From ragged clouds the moon burst forth to view.

With crystal towers and glittering battlement,
   A pictured castle in the moonlight gleamed,
In silver set, a gem of Occident,
   Like clustered starry jewels brightly beamed.

Now, when the Winter Spirit's fair design,
   In beauty rare, complete before him lay,
"Farewell," he sighed, "the frosty gem be thine!
   While I in storm and darkness fly away."

Once more to darkling storm the night was given,
   Once more the wild wind whistled through the town,
Like myriad blessings sent to earth from Heaven,
   The air was thick with snowflakes coming down.

SNOWSHOEING SONG.

Arthur Weir.

Hilloo, hilloo, hilloo, hilloo;
Gather, gather ye men in white;
The winds blow keenly, the moon is bright,
The sparkling snow lies firm and white;
Tie on the shoes, no time to lose,
We must be over the hill to-night.

Hilloo, hilloo, hilloo, hilloo;
Swiftly in single file we go,
The city is soon left far below,
Its countless lights like diamonds glow;
And as we climb we hear the chime
Of church bells stealing o'er the snow.

Hilloo, hilloo, hilloo, hilloo;
Like winding-sheet about the dead,
O'er hill and dale the snow is spread,
And silences our hurried tread;
The pines bend low, and to and fro
The magpies toss their boughs o'erhead.

Hilloo, hilloo, hilloo, hilloo;
We laugh to scorn the angry blast,
The mountain top is gained and past.
Descent begins, 'tis ever fast—
One short quick run, and toil is done,
We reach the welcome inn at last.

Shake off, shake off the clinging snow;
Unloose the shoe, the sash untie,
Fling tuque and mittens lightly by,
The chimney fire is blazing high,
And, richly stored, the festive board
Awaits the merry company.

Remove the fragments of the feast!
The steaming coffee, waiter, bring.
Now tell the tale, the chorus sing,
And let the laughter loudly ring;
Here's to our host, drink down the toast,
Then up! for time is on the wing.

Hilloo, hilloo, hilloo, hilloo;
The moon is sinking out of sight,
Across the sky dark clouds take flight,
And dimly looms the mountain height;
Tie on the shoes, no time to lose,
We must be home again to-night.

SKATING.

John Lowry Stuart.

Come to the moonlit lake,
  Where rays of silver bright
Their slender arrows break
  On the glassy pavement bright!
For hearts are gay, and joy is rife;
And youth and beauty, love and life,
  Are out on the ice to-night.

Not in the crowded hall,
  Where earth-lit tapers gleam,
We'll hold our festival,
  But out on the frozen stream;
No dull faint air, or heated room,
Shall rob thy cheek of beauty's bloom,
  Thine eye of its sparkling beam.

Bright is the fairy scene;
  The ringing steels resound;
And gleams the glowing sheen
  To feet of beauty bound;
And health, with rosy pencil, seeks
To paint the blush on beauty's cheeks,
  And the echoing laugh rings round.

Ne'er such a pavement spread
  Glittered in marble halls;
Ne'er gleamed such lamps o'erhead
  To gladden their carnivals;
The circling hills, whose tree-clad brows
Upbear the dome on cornice boughs,
  Are our lofty palace walls.

Whence foaming waters roar
  That winter could not bind
(Their brothers called on Huron's shore,
  And they would not stay confined).
As free and gay, and wild as they,
We'll speed e'en to the mystic way
  Of the isle with cedars lined.

Earth and its cares forgot,
  Our hearts we'll then reveal;
And spurn each colder thought,
  As the ice the flashing steel.
Who, 'neath the sway of Luna's ray,
Love's sweet commands could disobey,
  Or its brighter beams conceal?

THE WINTER CARNIVAL.

John Reade.

I.

We fear thee not, O Winter !
  Though stern thy face and grim ;
Though vast thy strength to crush and rend
  Our bodies, limb from limb.
On Scandinavian mountains,
  On stormy northern seas,
Our fathers braved thy wrath of yore,
And heeded not thy sullen roar
  Amid the bending trees.

II.

They loved thy gusty music,
  And from full chests and throats
Rivalled, in happy recklessness,
  The Storm-King's boisterous notes ;
They made thee now their playmate,
  They made thee now their slave ;
Thy frost-built roads for them to ride,
With fair-haired lemans side by side,
  Above the rushing wave.

III.

Over the snows they trod apace,
  Adown the drifts they sped ;
They met thy fury face to face,
  And all thy shapes of dread.

And though thy wild sport sometimes left
   Sights that were sad to see,
Health, beauty, courage, giant thews,
Well braced by salutary use,
   Came of their fight with thee.

IV.

Such were the hardy Northmen,
   By land and sea renowned;
Such gifts they brought where'er their feet
   New resting-places found.
Such gifts to France, to England,
   To Scotia's shores, they brought;
And many a thrice-encircled rath
Still shows on Erin's hills the path
   By which they came and fought.

V.

Such gifts to this new Northland
   All we of Northern blood,
Tempered by other gentler strains,
   Brought with us o'er the flood
To this broad land, where Winter
   Is Summer's best ally;
And with his robe, so soft and white,
Her tender children shields from blight
   Beneath the brumal sky.

VI.

Ages ago, in battle,
   We fairly won the day;
And, though we still may call him king,
   He bears disputed sway.

We make his mighty forces
   Obedient to our will;
Beneath our hands his ice and snow
To wondrous shapes of beauty grow,
   Triumphs of art and skill.

VII.

Out of his frozen torrents
   We carve the glittering mass,
And raise a dome, whose fairy charms
   Old Greece could not surpass.
Upon its fair proportions
   Men gaze in silent awe,
As those who in a dream behold
The streets of pearl and gates of gold
   Which John in Patmos saw.

VIII.

And who that loveth Nature
   Feels not his heart aglow
In presence of our winter woods,
   Tinselled with ice and snow!
'Twas just such woodland visions,
   With moonlight glimmering down,
Gave pious hearts the rapt desire
To raise the grand cathedral spire
   In many a feudal town.

IX.

O Winter! if thy anger
   Affrights the poor of heart,
Best humoured and most cheery
   Of playfellows thou art.

E'en Summer cannot rival
　　Thy many-sided glee;
For young and old, for maid and boy,
Thou hast a store of healthy joy
　　To bind our hearts to thee.

x.

Now, in thy festal season,
　　We celebrate thy praise;
For our Canadian Carnival
　　Send us auspicious days.
All ills that flesh is heir to
　　Be banished from our train;
And may the pleasures of the scene
Keep in each heart its memory green
　　Until we meet again!

THE SPIRIT OF THE CARNIVAL.

"FLEURANGE."

ONWARD! the people shouted,
　　Let merriment be king!
Fling out your crimson banners,
　　Your fragrant roses fling,—
Fly faster, maddened horses,
　　Through din of trumpets loud;
Crash down the dusty Corso,
　　Cheered by the frantic crowd!

Sweep onward, gaudy pageant,
   In wild uproarious glee;
Dark goblins, elves fantastic,
   Strange shapes from land and sea;
Wave high the flaming torches!
   Clang loud the brazen bells!
The great enchanter, Carnival,
   Hath Rome within his spells.

Weary of heat and clamour
   A young Italian lay
Beneath the ilex shadow,
   When closed the burning day;
Faint as his faded garlands
   His drowsy eyelids seem,—
The Spirit of the Carnival,
   Comes to him in his dream:

"Awake, oh youth, arouse thee,
   And follow where I lead;
I know thy ardent nature,
   Thy soul is strong indeed;
It loathes the gilded folly,
   The childish pranks and play,
The weak excited populace
   Wild with a holiday.

"And here, indeed, *I* linger
   To laugh and jest awhile;
But as a king may pause to greet
   A wilful beauty's smile.

Yet guardeth ever in his heart
　　An image pure and fair,
And hastening homeward to his queen
　　Finds life and love are there,—

"So follow, follow where I lead,
　　Across the western sea,
Where thou shalt learn thy manhood might,
　　From farce and folly free."
The youth sighed in his sleep—his soul
　　Obeyed the strange command,—
The great enchanter, Carnival,
　　Still led him by the hand.

And soon the groves of olives
　　Are fading from his sight,
The dim blue shores of Italy
　　Melt into deeper night;
Fresh draughts of light inhaling,
　　Where northern breezes blow,
Vast regions lie before him
　　All white with frost and snow.

"Behold!" th' enchanter whispered,
　　"Gaze on, and thou shalt see
Why Canada, my kingdom,
　　My chosen home should be;
Here all my sports and merriment,
　　To noble ends allied,
Teach manly strength and fortitude,
　　A nation's truest pride.

See ! like a jewel burning
   Upon a silver band,
Fair Montreal is shining
   Upon the snowy land ;
Its stately mansions glowing
   With hospitable cheer,
The merry sleigh-bells ringing
   Re-echo far and near."

The city keeps high festival,
   The icy air, like wine,
Quickens each pace to bounding glee,
   Bright eyes with gladness shine.
With merry laughter following fast
   From countless summits high—
Like flashing arrows from a bow,
   The swift toboggans fly !

Then, as the youth gazed on, he sees
   A fairy palace rise,
Seeming of mist and moonbeams born,
   Or poet's fantasies ;
Within it throbs a soul of fire,
   That glows through every part,
Softly as shines the light of love
   Within a maiden's heart.

A moment, and the magic scene
   Grows strangely bright as day,
For, see ! an army storms the fort,
   Oh, guard it while ye may !

Hurrah! the rockets leap aloft,
　　The waving torches flare—
A rainbow shower of golden stars
　　Breaks into glory there!

And far on yonder mountain side
　　A chain of living light!
Each link a stalwart snow-shoer
　　With torch that blazes bright,—
A jewelled order proudly flung
　　On old Mount Royal's breast,
A starry circlet from the skies
　　Dropt on his snowy crest.

Then lights and city faded,
　　And the dreamer woke at last,
O'er him hung the old-world languor,
　　Faint with mem'ries of the past;
But his spirit glowed within him,
　　And he left the careless throng,
Lived and wrought in earnest fashion,
　　Toil or pastime, brave and strong.

So may faint hearts ever gather
　　From Canadian sports and play
Something of the force that, working,
　　Hewed the forests, cleared the way:
For the tree shows fairer blossom
　　Where the roots are wide and deep,
And the pleasure turns to glory
　　When the victors revel keep;

And the Carnival no longer wears
   The bells as Fancy's Fool,—
He is a King, whose subjects free,
   Are loyal to his rule;
Each merry heart beats true and fast,
   And knows, amid his play,
To-morrow he can meet the foe
   Who tries his strength to-day.

Then guard it well, fair Canada,
   Thy festival of snow,
Proving old winter, stern and grim,
   Thy friend and not thy foe;
And may thy sons build steadfastly
   A nation great and free,
Whose vast foundations stretch abroad
   From mighty sea to sea.

Long may Canadians bear thy name
   In unity and pride,—
Their progress, like thy rushing streams,
   Roll a resistless tide;
Their hearts be tender as the flowers
   That o'er thy valleys grow,
Their courage rugged as thy frost
   When winds of winter blow;
Their honour brilliant as thy skies,
   And stainless as thy snow!

VII.—The Spirit of Canadian History.

VII.—THE SPIRIT OF CANADIAN HISTORY.

JACQUES CARTIER.

Hon. Thomas D'Arcy M'Gee.

In the seaport of St. Malo, 'twas a smiling morn in May,
When the Commodore Jacques Cartier to the westward sailed away;
In the crowded old Cathedral, all the town were on their knees,
For the safe return of kinsmen from the undiscovered seas;
And every autumn blast that swept o'er pinnacle and pier,
Filled many hearts with sorrow, and gentle hearts with fear.

A year passed o'er St. Malo—again came round the day,
When the Commodore Jacques Cartier to the westward sailed away;
But no tidings from the absent had come the way they went.

And tearful were the vigils that many a maiden spent;
And manly hearts were filled with gloom, and gentle hearts with fear,
When no tidings came from Cartier at the closing of the year.

But the earth is as the Future, it hath its hidden side,
And the Captain of St. Malo was rejoicing in his pride;
In the forests of the North—while his townsmen mourned his loss—
He was rearing on Mount Royal the *fleur-de-lis* and cross;
And when two months were over, and added to the year,
St. Malo hailed him home again, cheer answering to cheer.

He told them of a region, hard, iron-bound, and cold,
Nor seas of pearl abounded, nor mines of shining gold;
Where the wind from Thulé freezes the word upon the lip,
And the ice in spring comes sailing athwart the early ship;
He told them of the frozen scene, until they thrilled with fear,
And piled fresh fuel on the hearth to make them better cheer.

But when he chang'd the strain,—he told how soon is cast
In early Spring, the fetters that hold the waters fast;
How the Winter causeway, broken, is drifted out to sea,
And the rills and rivers sing with pride the anthem of the free;

How the magic wand of Summer clad the landscape to
    his eyes,
Like the dry bones of the just when they wake in
    Paradise.

He told them of the Algonquin braves—the hunters of
    the wild;
Of how the Indian mother in the forest rocks her child;
Of how, poor souls, they fancy in every living thing
A spirit good or evil, that claims their worshipping;
Of how they brought their sick and maim'd for him to
    breathe upon;
And of the wonders wrought for them, thro' the Gospel
    of St. John.

He told them of the river, whose mighty current gave
Its freshness for a hundred leagues to ocean's briny
    wave;
He told them of the glorious scene presented to his sight,
What time he reared the cross and crown on Hochelaga's
    height;
And of the fortress cliff, that keeps of Canada the key;—
And they welcomed back Jacques Cartier from the perils
    over sea.

THE CAPTURED FLAG.

Arthur Weir.

Loudly roared the English cannon, loudly thundered back our own,
Pouring down a hail of iron from their battlements of stone,
Giving Frontenac's proud message to the clustered British ships:
"I will answer your commander only by my cannons' lips."
Through the sulphurous smoke below us, on the Admiral's ship of war,
Faintly gleamed the British ensign, as through cloud-wrack gleams a star;
And above our noble fortress, on Cape Diamond's rugged crest,—
Like a crown upon a monarch, like an eagle in its nest,—
Streamed our silken flag, emblazoned with the royal *fleur-de-lys*,
Flinging down a proud defiance to the rulers of the sea.
As we saw it waving proudly, and beheld the crest it bore,
Fiercely throbbed our hearts within us, and with bitter words we swore,
While the azure sky was reeling at the thunder of our guns,
We would strike that standard never, while Old France had gallant sons.

Long and fiercely raged the struggle, oft our foes had sought to land,
But with shot and steel we met them, met and drove them from the strand;

Though they owned them not defeated, and the stately Union Jack,
Streaming from the slender topmast, seemed to wave them proudly back.
Louder rose the din of combat, thicker rolled the battle smoke,
Through whose murky folds the crimson tongues of thundering cannon broke;
And the ensign sank and floated in the smoke-clouds on the breeze,
As a wounded fluttering sea-bird floats upon the stormy seas.
While we looked upon it sinking, rising through the sea of smoke,
Lo! it shook, and bending downwards, as a tree beneath a stroke,
Hung one moment o'er the river, then precipitously fell,
Like proud Lucifer descending from high heaven into hell.
As we saw it flutter downwards, till it reached the eager wave,
Not Cape Diamond's loudest echo could have matched the cheer we gave;
Yet the English, still undaunted, sent an answering echo back;
Though their flag had fallen conquered, still their fury did not slack,
And with louder voice their cannon to our cannonade replied,
As their tattered ensign drifted slowly shoreward with the tide.

There was one who saw it floating, and within his heart of fire,
Beating in a Frenchman's bosom, rose at once a fierce desire,

That the riven flag thus resting on the broad St. Lawrence tide
Should, for years to come, betoken how France humbled England's pride.
As the stag leaps down the mountain, with the baying hounds in chase,
So the hero, swift descending, sought Cape Diamond's rugged base,
And within the water, whitened by the bullets' deadly hail,
Springing, swam towards the ensign with a stroke that could not fail.
From the shore and from the fortress we looked on with bated breath,
For around him closer, closer, fell the messengers of death;
And as nearer, ever nearer, to the floating flag he drew,
Thicker round his head undaunted still the English bullets flew.
He has reached and seized the trophy. Ah! what cheering rent the skies,
Mingled with deep English curses, as he shoreward brought his prize!
Slowly, slowly, almost sinking, still he struggled to the land,
And we hurried down to meet him as he reached the welcome strand;
Proudly up the rock we bore him, with the flag that he had won,
And that night the English vessels left us with the setting sun.

HOW CANADA WAS SAVED.

(May 1660.)

GEORGE MURRAY.

"Il faut ici donner la gloire à ces dix-sept François de Montréal, et honorer leurs cendres d'un éloge qui leur est deu avec justice, et que nous ne pouvons leur refuser sans ingratitude. Tout estait perdu, s'ils n'eussent péri, et leur malheur a sauvé ce païs."—RELATIONS DES JESUITES, 1660, p. 17.

BESIDE the dark Utawa's stream, two hundred years ago,
A wondrous feat of arms was wrought, which all the world should know:
'Tis hard to read with tearless eyes that record of the past,
It stirs the blood, and fires the soul, as with a clarion's blast.
What though no blazoned cenotaph, no sculptured columns, tell
Where the stern heroes of my song, in death triumphant, fell;
What though beside the foaming flood untombed their ashes lie,
All earth becomes the monument of men who nobly die.

A score of troublous years had passed since on Mount-Royal's crest
The gallant Maisonneuve upreared the Cross devoutly bless'd,
And many of the saintly Guild that founded Ville-Marie
With patriot pride had fought and died—determined to be free.

Fiercely the Iroquois had sworn to sweep, like grains of sand,
The Sons of France from off the face of their adopted land,
When, like the steel that oft disarms the lightning of its power,
A fearless few their country saved in danger's darkest hour.

Daulac, the Captain of the Fort—in manhood's fiery prime—
Hath sworn by some immortal deed to make his name sublime,
And sixteen "Soldiers of the Cross," his comrades true and tried,
Have pledged their faith for life and death—all kneeling side by side;
And this their oath:—On flood or field, to challenge face to face
The ruthless hordes of Iroquois, the scourges of their race;
No quarter to accept or grant,—and, loyal to the grave,
To die like martyrs for the land they shed their blood to save.

Shrived by the priest within the Church where oft they had adored,
With solemn fervour they partake the Supper of the Lord;
And now, those self-devoted youths from weeping friends have passed,
And on the Fort of Ville-Marie each fondly looks his last.

Unskilled to steer the frail canoe, or stem the rushing tide,
On through a virgin wilderness, o'er stream and lake they glide,
Till, weary of the paddle's dip, they moor their barks below
A Rapid of Utawa's flood—the turbulent Long-Sault.

There, where a grove of gloomy pines sloped gently to the shore,
A moss-grown Palisade was seen—a Fort in days of yore;
Fenced by its circle, they encamped; and on the listening air,
Before those staunch Crusaders slept, arose the voice of prayer.
Sentry and scout kept watch and ward, and soon, with glad surprise,
They welcomed to their roofless hold a band of dark allies,—
Two stalwart chiefs and forty "braves"—all sworn to strike a blow
In one great battle for their lives against the common foe.

Soft was the breath of balmy Spring in that fair month of May,
The wild flower bloomed, the wild bird sang on many a budding spray,—
A tender blue was in the sky, on earth a tender green,
And Peace seemed brooding, like a dove, o'er all the sylvan scene;

When, loud and high, a thrilling cry dispelled the magic charm,
And scouts came hurrying from the woods to bid their comrades arm,
And bark canoes skimmed lightly down the torrent of the Sault,
Manned by three hundred dusky forms—the long expected foe.

They spring to land—a wilder brood hath ne'er appalled the sight—
With carbines, tomahawks, and knives that gleam with baleful light;
Dark plumes of eagles crest their chiefs, and broidered deerskins hide
The blood-red war-paint that shall soon a bloodier red be dyed.
Hark! to the death-song that they chant,—behold them as they bound,
With flashing eyes and vaunting tongues, defiantly around;
Then, swifter than the wind, they fly the barrier to invest,
Like hornet-swarms that heedless boys have startled from a nest.

As Ocean's tempest-driven waves dash forward on a rock,
And madly break in seething foam, hurl'd backward by the shock,
So onward dashed that surging throng, so backward were they hurl'd,
When from the loopholes of the Fort flame burst and vapour curl'd.

Each bullet aimed by bold Daulac went crashing through
   the brain,
Or pierced the bounding heart of one who never stirred
   again;
The trampled turf was drenched with blood—blood
   stained the passing wave—
It seemed a carnival of death, the harvest of the grave.

The sun went down—the fight was o'er—but sleep was
   not for those
Who, pent within that frail redoubt, sighed vainly for
   repose;
The shot that hissed above their heads, the Mohawks'
   taunting cries,
Warned them that never more on earth must slumber
   seal their eyes.
In that same hour their swart allies, o'erwhelmed by
   craven dread,
Leaped o'er the parapet like deer and traitorously fled;
And, when the darkness of the night had vanished, like
   a ghost,
Twenty and two were left—of all—to brave a maddened
   host.

Foiled for a time, the subtle foes have summoned to their
   aid
Five hundred kinsmen from the Isles, to storm the
   Palisade;
And, panting for revenge, they speed, impatient for the
   fray,
Like birds of carnage from their homes allured by scent
   of prey.

With scalp-locks streaming in the breeze, they charge,
   —but never yet
Have legions in the storm of fight a bloodier welcome
   met
Than those doomed warriors, as they faced the desolating
   breath
Of wide-mouthed musketoons that poured hot cataracts
   of death.

Eight days of varied horrors passed ! What boots it now
   to tell
How the pale tenants of the Fort heroically fell ?
Hunger, and thirst, and sleeplessness—death's ghastly
   aids—at length
Marred and defaced their comely forms, and quelled their
   giant strength.
The end draws nigh—they yearn to die—one glorious
   rally more
For the dear sake of Ville-Marie, and all will soon be
   o'er;
Sure of the martyr's golden Crown, they shrink not from
   the Cross,
Life yielded for the land they love they scorn to reckon
   loss !

The Fort is fired, and through the flames, with slippery,
   splashing tread,
The Redmen stumble to the camp o'er ramparts of the
   dead ;
There, with set teeth and nostril wide, Daulac the
   dauntless stood,
And dealt his foes remorseless blows 'mid blinding
   smoke and blood,

Till, hacked and hewn, he reeled to earth, with proud unconquered glance,
Dead—but immortalised by death—Leonidas of France!
True to their oath, that glorious band no quarter basely craved ;—
So died the peerless Twenty-two, so Canada was saved!

MADELEINE DE VERCHÈRES.

JOHN READE.

I.

"OH ! my country, bowed in anguish 'neath a weight of bitter woe,
Who shall save thee from the vengeance of the desolating foe?
They have sworn a heathen oath, that every Christian soul must die,—
God of Heaven, in mercy shield us ! Father, hear thy children's cry."

II.

Thus prayed Madeleine, the daughter of an old heroic line,—
Grecian poet, had he seen her, would have deemed her race divine ;
But as the golden sun transcends the beauty of the brightest star,
Than all the charms of face or form her maiden heart was lovelier far.

III.

We can see her now in fancy, through the dim years
    gazing back
To those stormy days of old, the days of valiant Fron-
    tenac,
When the thinly settled land was sadly wasted far and
    near,
And before the savage foe the people fled like stricken
    deer.

IV.

'Tis the season when the forest wears its many-coloured
    dress,
And a strange foreboding whisper answers back the
    wind's caress
As the swaying pines repeat the murmurs of the distant
    waves,
While the children of the Summer flutter softly to their
    graves.

V.

But—was that another whisper, warning *her* of ill to
    come,
As she stands beside the river, near her father's fortress-
    home?
Hark! the sound of stealthy footsteps creeps upon the
    throbbing ear—
Maiden, fly! the foe approaches, and no human aid is
    near.

VI.

Surely He who decked with beauty this fair earth on which we dwell,
Never meant that men should change it by their madness into hell !
He who gave the trees their glory, gave the birds their gift of song,
Cannot smile from out yon heavens at the sight of human wrong.

VII.

But those savage hearts no beauty wins to thoughts of tender ruth—
Mother fond, or gentle maid, or smiling innocence of youth.
See ! with fierce exulting yells the flying maiden they pursue—
Hear her prayer, O God, and save her from that wild vindictive crew.

VIII.

Never ere that day or since was such a race by maiden run,
Never 'gainst such fearful odds was wished-for goal so swiftly won ;
Fifty foes are on her track, the bullets graze her floating hair—
But worse than vain is all their rage, for God above has heard her prayer.

IX.

Madeleine has reached the Fort,—the gates are closed against the foe,
But now, a stricken throng sends up to heaven a wail of woe—
Feeble men, and fainting women, without heart or hope or plan—
Then it was that God gave courage to a maid to act the man.

X.

Then it was that Madeleine bethought her of her father's name:
"Never shall a soldier's daughter die the coward's death of shame;
Never in the days to come, when Canada is great and proud,
Be it said a Christian maiden by a heathen's threat was cowed.

XI.

"He is but a craven wretch would bid me yield in such an hour—
Never yet my country's sons in peril's face were known to cower!
No, my people! God is with us; 'tis our homes that we defend—
Let the savage do his worst, we will oppose him to the end.

XII.

"Women, I am but a girl, but heroes' blood is in my veins,
And I will shed it drop by drop before I see my land in chains;
Let them tear me limb from limb, or strew my ashes to the wind,
Ere I disgrace the name I bear, or leave a coward's fame behind.

XIII.

"Brothers mine, though young in years, you are old enough to know
That to shed your blood is noble, fighting with your country's foe!
Be the lesson unforgotten that our noble father gave,
Whether glory be its guerdon, or it wins us but a grave.

XIV.

"Come, my people, take your places, every one as duty calls;
Death to every foe who ventures to approach these fortress walls!
Let no point be unprotected, leave the rest to God on high,
That we shall have done our duty, even if we have to die."

XV.

Thus she raised their drooping courage, matchless maiden, Madeleine,
And the cry, "To arms!" re-echoed, till the roof-trees rang again;
Cannons thundered, muskets rattled, and the clank of steel was heard,
Till the baffled foe retreated, like a wolf untimely scared.

XVI.

Seven days and seven nights, with sleepless eye and bated breath,
They held the Fort against the foe that lurked around them plotting death!
At last a joyous challenge came, it was the brave La Monnerie,
And up to heaven arose a shout, "The foe has fled, and we are free."

THE BATTLE OF LA PRAIRIE.

(1691.)

(*A Ballad.*)

WILLIAM DOUW LIGHTHALL.

I.

THAT was a brave old epoch,
  Our age of chivalry,
When the Briton met the Frenchman
  At the Fight of La Prairie;
And the manhood of New England,
  And the Netherlanders true,
And Mohawks sworn, gave battle
  To the Bourbon's lilied blue.

II.

That was a brave old Governor,
  Who mustered his array,
And stood to meet, he knew not what,
  On that alarming day.
Eight hundred, against rumours vast
  That filled the wild wood's gloom,
With all New England's flower of youth,
  Fierce for New France's doom.

III.

And the brave old scarce three hundred!
  Theirs should in truth be fame;
Borne down the savage Richelieu
  On what emprise they came!

Your hearts are great enough, O few:
   Only your numbers fail!
New France asks more for conquerors,
   All glorious though your tale.

IV.

It was a brave old battle,
   That surged around the fort,
When D'Hosta fell in charging,
   And 'twas deadly strife and short;
When in the very quarters
   They contested face and hand,
And many a goodly fellow
   Crimsoned yon La Prairie sand

V.

And those were brave old orders
   The colonel gave to meet
That forest force, with trees entrenched,
   Opposing the retreat:
" De Callières' strength's behind us,
   And beyond's your Richelieu:
We must go straightforth at them;
   There is nothing else to do."

VI.

And then the brave old story comes,
   Of Schuyler and Valrennes,*
When " Fight ! " the British colonel called,
   Encouraging his men,

   * Pronounced "Skyler" and "Valrenn."

"For the Protestant Religion,
  And the honour of our King!"--
"Sir, I am here to answer you!"
  Valrennes cried, forthstepping.

VII.

Were those not brave old races?—
  Well, here they still abide;
And yours is one or other,
  And the second's at your side.
So when you hear your brother say,
  "Some loyal deed I'll do;"
Like old Valrennes, be ready with,
  "I'm here to answer you!"

THE BATTLE OF GRAND PRÉ.

(February 9th, 1746.)

M. J. KATZMANN LAWSON.

Room for the dead, the honoured dead, in this fair year
    of grace;
In the Valhalla of the brave, give them a glorious place!
The loyal men who crossed the sea, and came with battle
    ring,
To hold this free fair land of ours a province for their
    king.

When winter's iron fetters bound river and lake and bay,
And snow-drifts, piled in fleecy white, on plain and
  mountain lay,
Where Blomidon's blue crest looks down upon the valley
  land,
And the great waves of Fundy lap the grey stones on the
  strand ;
Here, where the scattered homesteads stood, from time
  and labour won,
The brave commander of the force quartered his garrison,
Retaining for his citadel the old French stone housé, set
Where the ripple of the Gaspereaux sighs round its ruins
  yet.

Down from the heights of Cobequid, on noiseless snow-
  shoes borne,
Slowly the crafty foeman came, by march and travel
  worn ;
Lightly the low toboggans swept, bearing their motley
  freight,
Food for the rebels on the march, shot for the brave who
  wait ;
Broad rivers, all unknown to name, their stealthy footsteps crossed,
The Shubenacadie, Ste. Croix, and Avon bridged by
  frost ;
For sixteen weary days they crept over these leagues of
  snow,
As the grim panther tracks his prey, so stole they on the
  foe.
In the deep stillness of the night,—out from the cold,
  black cloud,
The snowflakes, falling one by one, the hemlock branches
  bowed ;

Forest, and plain, and hamlet, all hushed in slumber
   deep,
And still before the driving blast the freezing Frenchmen
   creep;
With panting breath and weary tread, through midnight's
   icy blast,
With murder in their hearts, they reach the Grand Pré
   camp at last.
The sentinels were at their post, within the watchers
   slept,
Hushed in the tumult which the storm and cruel snow-
   drift kept;
Oh, God! that brave men thus should die, no time to
   rouse or stir!
One hundred English soldiers fell in that dread massacre,
Guarding the colours of their king in this new province
   land,—
Scalped by the Indians' tomahawk, hewn down by alien
   hand!

Roused by the din at dead of night, piercing the stone
   house then,
Brave Noble faced, with sword in hand, those fierce and
   blood-stained men;
The bitter wind in fury swept around his half-clad form,
And flash of steel and sweep of shot, more cruel than the
   storm;
The Red Cross flag of England waved above his fortress
   rude,
And brave, as all her loyal sons, he well her foes with-
   stood;
All worn and faint, from battle sore, wounded in heart
   and frame,
From dying lips the valiant shout of "No surrender!"
   came.

Nor nobler names can Britain write upon her glorious
    scroll
Than those who held the fort that night where Minas'
    waters roll,—
Surprised, and overpowered and slain, yet heroes every
    one,
Those cold, set faces, white and still, turned to the rising
    sun.
Though many a score of years has marked this earth with
    loss and gain,
Since Noble fought his last long fight on Grand Pré's
    snowy plain,
No stone is raised to mark the place where his brave
    comrades fell,
No monument above his grave, of valiant deeds to tell.
Room for the honoured dead to-day, in memory's tender
    grace.
To chronicle their glorious deeds above their burial-
    place.
Crimean heroes, all our own, Lucknow and Kars still tell
That Nova Scotia's sons can serve their Queen and
    country well!
But, with their fame, let us recall the battle long ago,
When English soldiers met the French at daybreak in the
    snow;
And held the fort, and kept the flag, as only heroes
    could,
Where, in this orchard land of ours, the old grey stone
    house stood.
Now, in this year of Jubilee, when living deeds are read,
Glance backward through the centuries which hold our
    honoured dead,—
Where Lechmere sank, and Pickering died, where the
    brave Noble fell,
Under our own old English flag, the flag they loved so well;

Where sunny Gaspereaux sweeps on amid the apple trees,
And the blue waves of Minas chant a requiem to the
    breeze;
Raise shaft or column to the dead, let some memorial fair
Tell to our children's children still that *Heroes* slumber
    there!

SPINA CHRISTI.

WILLIAM KIRBY.

PART I.

> "There is a thorn—it looks so old,
> In truth you'd find it hard to say
> How it could ever have been young,
> It looks so old and grey."
>   —WORDSWORTH.

THE city walls of Avignon are built of stone, and high
The houses stand, with balconies above the streets that
    lie
Around the old cathedral, whose sweet bells were ringing
    clear
A merry tune, one day in June
Of seventeen hundred year,
And half a hundred years beside, while crowding far and
    near,
Beneath the flags and tapestries, the people loudly
    cheer;—
The regiment of Rousillon is ordered to the war,
A thousand strong, the pick among
The mountaineers of Var.

The great Church portals open wide, the crowd goes
    surging in,
The soldiers tramp with measured tread—the services
    begin,
A blessing is invoked upon the King's Canadian war;
Beyond the seas there is no ease,
And all things are ajar.
The English in America do boldly break and mar
The peace they made; but we will keep the treaties as
    they are!
And now the Royal Rousillon take up the route with joy,
And march away while bugles play—
'Mid shouts of "Vive le Roy!"

There lives a lady beautiful as any Provence rose,
The chatelaine of Bois le Grand, who weepeth as she
    goes—
For sleep has left her eyelids on the banks of rapid Rhone:
"But three months wed! alas," she said,
"To live my life alone!
Pining for my dear husband, in his old chateau of stone,
While he goes with his regiment, and I am left to moan;
That his dear head, so often laid at rest upon my knee,
No pillow kind, but stones, shall find—
No shelter but a tree!"

"Weep not, dear wife!" replied the count, and took
    her in his arms,
And kissed her lovingly, and smiled to quiet her alarms;
They stood beneath the holy thorn of the old Celestine,
Pope Clement brought with blessing fraught
And planted it between
The wall and wall beside the cross, where he was daily
    seen

To kneel before it reverently. It came from Palestine,
A plant from that which cruelly the crown of thorns supplied,
Christ wore for me, when mocked was He,
And scourged and crucified.

"I'll take a branch of it," he said, "across the stormy sea
That roars between New France and Old, and plant it solemnly
In that far country where I go campaigning for the King;
It will remind and teach mankind
Of pains that blessing bring."
Above his head he plucked a spray acute with many a sting,
And placed it on his plumed chapeau, in token of the thing
Alone can turn the sinful man—the piercing of the thorn—
The healing smart—the contrite heart—
Of penitence new born.

Despairingly she kissed his lips: "O welcome sharpest pain,
That cuts the heart to bleeding, and bids hope revive again!
O Spina Christi! to my heart I press thee wet with tears—
If love outlast as in the past
Each parting that endears!
Our sky has been so bright and filled with music of the spheres,
So gloomy now in sad eclipse it suddenly appears!

For joy dies out in silence like sweet singing that is
    done,
If men forget their sacred debt
To women they have won."

PART II.

Atlantic gales come winged with clouds and voices of the
    sea,
The misty Capes uncap to hear the ocean melody;
In broad St. Lawrence rise and fall the everlasting tides,
Which come and go with ebb and flow—
While every ship that rides
At anchor swings, and east or west the passing flood
    divides,
Or westward ho! 'mid seamen's shouts still onward
    gently glides,
Tasting the waters sweet from lakes, of boundless soli-
    tude
Where thousand isles break into smiles
Of nature's gladdest mood.

    .   .   .   .

A hundred leagues and many more towards the glowing
    west,
Amid the forests' silence, Ontario lay at rest—
Keel rarely ploughed, or paddle dipt its wilderness of blue;
Where day by day life passed away
In peace that irksome grew.
In old Niagara fort, a cross stood loftily in view,*

---

* In the centre of the fort stood a cross eighteen feet high, with the inscription "Regn. Vinc. Imp. Chrs." The interpretation of which admits of as much ambiguity as a Delphic oracle.

And *Regnat. Vincit. Imperat. Christus* the words did
    show
Carved on it, when the Rousillon came up in early spring
To close the port, and guard the fort,
And keep it for the King.

O! fair in summer time it is, Niagara plain to see,
Half belted round with oaken woods and green as grass
    can be!
Its levels broad in sunshine lie, with flowerets gemmed
    and set
With daisy stars, and red as Mars
The tiny sanguinet,
The trefoil with its drops of gold, white clover heads, and
    yet
The sweet grass, commonest of all God's goodnesses we
    get!
The dent-de-lions downy globes a puff will blow away,
Which children pluck to try good luck,
Or tell the time of day.

Count Bois le Grand sought out a spot of loveliness, was
    full
Of sandworts, silvered leaf and stem, with down of fairy
    wool;
Hard by the sheltering grove of oak he set the holy
    thorn,
Where still it grows and ever shows
How sharp the crown of scorn
Christ wore for man, reminding him what pain for sin
    was borne,
And warning him he must repent before his sheaf is
    shorn,

When comes the reaper, Death, and his last hour of life
    is scored,
Of all bereft, and only left
The mercy of the Lord.

The thorn was planted, leafed and bloomed, as if its sap
    were blood
That stained its berries crimson which fell dropping where
    it stood,
And seeded others like it,—as on Golgotha befell,
An awful sight, if seen aright,
The trees that root in hell ! *
Contorted, twisted, writhing, as with human pain to tell
Of cruel spines and agonies that God alone can quell.
A cluster like them Dante saw, and never after smiled;
A grove of doom, amid whose gloom
Were wicked souls exiled.

   .   .   .   .

Niagara fort was bravely built with bulwarks strong and
    high,
A tower of stone, and pallisades with ditches deep and
    dry,
And best of all behind them lay Guienne and Rousillon,†
La Sarre and Béarn, 'neath Pouchot stern—
A wall of men like stone—
De Villiers and Bois le Grand of old Avignon;

    * A number of these thorns, old and weird of aspect, are still standing on the plains of Niagara near the grove of Paradise; they were formerly called the "French thorns," a designation now nearly forgotten.
    † Portions of the regiments of Rousillon, La Sarre, Béarn, and Guienne formed the garrison of Niagara during the memorable siege of 1759.

And over all, the flag of France waved proudly in the
    sun.
Prepared for it—they met the war with gaiety and zest—
And every day barred up the way
That opened to the west.

Discord was rampant now and hate, and peace lay like a
    yoke,
That galled the necks of both of them, and French and
    English broke,
With mutual wrath and rivalry, the treaty they had
    made;
Too proud to live and each one give
Sunshine as well as shade.
From Louisburg to Illinois they stood as foes arrayed,
And east and west war's thunder rolled,—the soldier's
    polished blade
Flashed 'mid the savage tomahawks that struck and
    never spared,
While fort and field alternate yield
The bloody laurels shared.

The clouds of war rolled redder from the north, and
    English pride
Was stung to desperation at the turning of the tide,
When Montcalm the heroic, wise in council—struck the
    blow,
Won Chouaguen, and conquered then
At Carillon the foe.
But with his very victories his armies melted slow.
No help from France obtained he—and his heart sank
    very low;

He knew that England's courage flames the fiercest in
    defeat,
And in the day she stands at bay
Most dangerous to meet.

"Help us, O France ! to save thy fair dominion in the
    west,
Which for thy sake we planted, and have carved thy
    royal crest
Of golden lilies on the rocks beside the streams that flow
From mountain rills and past the hills
Of far-off Ohio ;
Then down leagues by the hundred, where bayous
    meander slow,
Through orange groves and sugar canes, and flowers that
    ever blow,
In fair Louisiana. We will take and hold the land
For Francia's crown of old renown,
If she will by us stand."

So spake Montcalm, and message sent—"My armies
    melt away
With victories—my beaten foes grow stronger every day;
In vain Monongahela and Carillon piled with slain,
If France forget to pay the debt
Of honour without stain,
She owes her sons who willingly are bleeding every vein
For sake of her white flag and crown, on fortress and on
    plain.
If we can keep Niagara safe that guards the western door,
Then in the east Quebec may feast
In quiet evermore."
Vain were Montcalm's appeals for aid, Voltaire's cold
    spirit ruled

The Court—while noisy doctrinaires a gallant nation
    schooled
In selfishness, and unbelief, and cowardice—and ease,
Which manhood daunt, while women flaunt
Their idle hours to please.
Degenerately they drank the wine of life mixed with the
    lees;
The Spartan virtues that make nations free and famous—
    these
Were mocked, derided, set at nought, while fatuous
    statesmen stand,
Whose feeble will, potent for ill,
Yields where it should command.

PART III.

Remote amid the trackless woods and waters of the west,
No enemy had broken yet Niagara's quiet rest.
The fifth year of the war came in—a change was nigh at
    hand;
The order ran to raise the ban
And make a final stand.
Prideaux and Johnson honoured were with new and high
    command,
From Albany a hundred leagues to march across the land,
While Wolfe besieged Quebec, and its defences battered
    in;
So they elate took bond of fate
Niagara to win.

But not before June's leafy days, when all the woods are
    green,
And skies are warm and waters clear, the English scouts
    were seen.

A lull before the tempest fell with weeks of steady calm,
Of golden hours when blooming flowers
Filled all the air with balm.
The garrison were now prepared to struggle for the palm,
To win the wreath of victory or die without a qualm;
So passed their time in jollity and ease, as if the day
Of bloody strife with life for life
Was continents away.

A fleet of swift canoes came up, all vocal with the song
Of voyageurs, whose cadences kept even time among
The dipping paddles, as they flashed along Ontario's
    shore,
Past headlands high and coasts that lie
In mistiness, and bore
A bevy of fair wives who loved their husbands more and
    more,—
Who could not bear their absence, and defiant of the roar
Of forests and of waters, came to comfort and caress,
As women may—and only they—
Man's solitariness.

In these Capuan days they basked in pleasure's sunny
    beams,
The Provence home of Bois le Grand was rarer in his
    dreams,
The chatelaine of his chateau fast by the rapid Rhone,
A memory dim became to him—
Nor loved he her alone.
A dame of charms most radiant—the cynosure that shone
Amid the constellations of Quebec's magnetic zone,

Drew him with force and held him fast, a captive with
    her eyes,
Which, dark and bright as tropic night,
Loved him without disguise;

And he remembered not the thorn he planted by the
    grove
Of Paradise, where he forgot in his forbidden love,
The chatelaine of Bois le Grand, the purest wife and best
Of womankind he left behind,
And ventured, like the rest,
To sport with woman's loveliness—as for a passing jest.
His heart was very lonely, too, while all beside were
    blest;
Like Samson in Delilah's lap, his lock of strength was
    shorn;
He loved again, despite the pain
And stinging of the thorn.

One day when he a-hunting went in the Norman Marsh,*
    and she
The dame he loved rode with him, as Diana fair to see
In green and silver habited, and silken bandoleer,
With dainty gun—by it undone!—
And bugle horn so clear;
While riding gaily up and down to turn the timid deer
And meet the joyance of his glance, when she should
    reappear,

---

* The "*Marais Normand*," so called during the French occupation of Niagara. It is now covered with farms, but is still called the swamp.

She vanished in the thicket, where a pretty stag had
    flown—
Saw something stir—alas for her!
She shot her lover down!

Bleeding he fell—"O, Madelaine!" his cry turned her
    to stone,
"What have you done unwittingly?" he uttered with a
    groan,
As she knelt over him with shrieks sky-rending, such as
    rise
From women's lips on sinking ships,
With death before their eyes.
She beat her breast despairingly; her hair dishevelled
    flies;
She kissed him madly, and in vain to stanch the blood
    she tries,
Till falling by him in a swoon they both lay as the
    dead—
A piteous sight! love's saddest plight!
With garments dabbled red.

Their servants ran, and hunters pale, and raised them
    from the ground;
Restored the dame to consciousness, and searched his
    fatal wound.
They pitched for him a spacious tent the river bank
    above,
With boundless care for ease and air
And tenderness of love.
She waited on him night and day; plucked off her silken
    glove
With self-accusing grief and tears—lamenting, as a dove

Bewails her wounded mate—so she—and in her bosom
   wore
A spike of thorn which every morn
She gathered—nothing more.

She cast her jewels off and dressed in robe of blackest
   hue,
Her face was pale as look the dead, and paler ever grew.
Smiles lit no more her rosy lips where sunbeams used to
   dance;
A withering blight that kills outright
Fell on her like a trance;
For Bois le Grand was dying, and it pierced her like a
   lance
To hear him vainly calling on his chatelaine in France,
And not for her who knelt by him, and lived but in his
   breath—
Remorse and grief without relief
Were hastening her death.

Far, far away in Avignon, beneath the holy thorn,
The chatelaine of Bois le Grand knelt down at eve and
   morn;
And prayed for him in hope and trust long witless of his
   fate;
But never knew he was untrue
And had repented late.
As caught between two seas his bark was in a rocky
   strait
And with his life went down the lives of those two
   women. Fate

Bedrugged the love, betrayed them both—and one by
    Laura's shrine
Took her last rest—the other best,
Drank death with him like wine.

Niagara's doom long threatened came—the roll of
    English drums
Was heard deep in the forest as Prideaux's stout army
    comes.
They sap and trench from day to day, the cannon fiercer
    roar,
The hot attack when beaten back
Again comes to the fore.
The pallisades are red with fire, the ramparts red with
    gore,
Its brave defenders on the walls die thickly more and
    more,
'Mid rack and ruin overwhelmed—no help above—below,
The few remain—not of the slain—
Surrender to the foe.

But not before all hope had fled, when gathered far and
    wide
From prairie, forest, fort, and field—with every tribe
    allied
To France, throughout the west they came, the fatal
    siege to raise,
And marched along, a mingled throng,
Amid the forest maze.
They halted in the meadows, where they stood like stags
    at gaze,
The English and the Iroquois confronting them for days,

Till Brant and Butler, wary chiefs, with stratagem of war
Broke up their host, and captured most,
While fled the rest afar.

The last day came, and Bois le Grand beheld with misty
    eyes
The flag of France run down the staff, and that of
    England rise.
It was the sharpest thorn of all that 'neath his pillow
    lay—
"O, Madelaine!" he cried, "my men!
My Rousillon so gay!
Fill graves of honour,—while I live to see this fatal day!
But not another! No!" he cried, and turned as cold as
    clay.
She kissed his mouth the last long kiss the dying get
    alone—
"O, Spina!" cried—fell by his side,
And both lay dead as stone.

THE LOYALISTS.

Sarah Anne Curzon.

O ye, who with your blood and sweat
    Watered the furrows of this land,—
See where upon a nation's brow,
    In honour's front, ye proudly stand!

Who for her pride abased your own,
    And gladly on her altar laid
All bounty of the older world,
    All memories that your glory made.

And to her service bowed your strength,
    Took labour for your shield and crest;
See where upon a nation's brow,
    Her diadem, ye proudly rest!

BROCK.

Charles Sangster.

One voice, one people, one in heart,
    And soul, and feeling, and desire!
    Re-light the smouldering martial fire,
    Sound the mute trumpet, strike the lyre,
    The hero deed can not expire,
        The dead still play their part.

Raise high the monumental stone!
    A nation's fealty is theirs,
    And we are the rejoicing heirs,
    The honoured sons of sires whose cares
    We take upon us unawares,
        As freely as our own.

We boast not of the victory,
    But render homage, deep and just,
    To his—to their—immortal dust,
    Who proved so worthy of their trust,
    No lofty pile nor sculptured bust
        Can herald their degree.

No tongue need blazon forth their fame,—
    The cheers that stir the sacred hill
    Are but mere promptings of the will
    That conquered then, that conquers still;
    And generations yet shall thrill
        At Brock's remembered name.

Some souls are the Hesperides
    Heaven sends to guard the golden age,
    Illuming the historic page
    With records of their pilgrimage;
    True Martyr, Hero, Poet, Sage:
        And he was one of these.

Each in his lofty sphere sublime
    Sits crowned above the common throng,
    Wrestling with some Pythonic wrong,
    In prayer, in thunder, thought, or song;
    Briareus-limbed, they sweep along,
        The Typhons of the time.

TECUMSEH'S DEATH.

Major Richardson.

Amid that scene, like some dark towering fiend,
   With death-black eyes and hands all spotted o'er,
The fierce Tecumseh on his tall lance leaned,
   Fired with much spoil and drunk with human gore;
And now his blasting glance ferocious gleamed—
   The chief who leads the eagles to his shore—
When, with one scream that devils might appal,
Deep in his breast he lodged the whizzing ball.

Like the quick bolt that follows on the flash
   Which rends the mountain oak in fearful twain,
So springs the warrior with infernal dash
   Upon the Christian writhing in his pain;
High gleamed his hatchet, ready now to crash
   Along the fibres of his swimming brain,
When from the adverse arm a bullet flew
With force resistless, and with aim too true.

The baffled Chieftain tottered, sunk, and fell,
   Rage in his heart, and vengeance in his glance;
His features ghastly pale—his breast was hell;
   One bound he made to seize his fallen lance,
But quick the death-shades o'er his vision swell,
   His arm dropped nerveless, straining to advance;
One look of hatred, and the last, he gave,
Then sunk and slumbered with the fallen brave.

Forth from the copse a hundred foemen spring,
    And pounce like vultures on the bleeding clay ;
Like famished bloodhounds to the corse they cling,
    And bear the fallen hero's spoils away ;
The very covering from his nerves they wring,
    And gash his form, and glut them o'er their prey,—
Wild hell-fiends all, and revelling at his death,
With bursting shrieks and pestilential breath.

A BALLAD FOR BRAVE WOMEN.

Charles Mair.

A STORY worth telling our annals afford,
'Tis the wonderful journey of Laura Secord !
Her poor crippled spouse hobbled home with the news,
That Bœrstler was nigh !   " Not a minute to lose,
Not an instant," said Laura, " for stoppage or pause—
I must hurry and warn our brave troops at Decaw's."
" What ! you ! " said her husband, " to famish and tire ! "
" Yes, me ! " said brave Laura, her bosom on fire.
" And how will you pass the gruff sentry," said he,
" Who is posted so near us ? "

                            " Just wait till you see ;
The foe is approaching, and means to surprise
Our troops, as you tell me.   Oh, husband, there flies

No dove with a message so needful as this—
I'll take it, I'll bear it. Good-bye, with a kiss."
Then a biscuit she ate, tucked her skirts well about,
And a bucket she slung on each arm, and went out.

'Twas the bright blush of dawn, when the stars melt
    from sight,
Dissolved by its breath like a dream of the night;
When Heaven seems opening on man and his pain,
Ere the rude day strengthens and shuts it again.
But Laura had eyes for her duty alone—
She marked not the glow and the gloom that were
    thrown
By the nurslings of morn, by the cloud-lands at rest,
By the spells of the East, and the weirds of the West.
Behind was the foe, full of craft and of guile;
Before her, a long day of travel and toil.
"No time this for gazing," said Laura, as near
To the sentry she drew.

                "Halt! You cannot pass here."
"I cannot pass here! Why, sirrah, you drowse,
Are you blind? Don't you see I am off to my cows?"
"Well, well, you can go." So she wended her way
To the pasture's lone side, where the farthest cow lay,
Got her up, caught a teat, and, with pail at her knees,
Made her budge, inch by inch, till she drew by degrees
To the edge of the forest. "I've hoaxed, on my word,
Both you and the sentry," said Laura Secord.

With a lingering look at her home, then away
She sped through the wild wood—a wilderness gray—

Nature's privacy, haunt of a virgin sublime,
And the mother who bore her, as ancient as Time;
Where the linden had space for its fans and its flowers,
The balsam its tents, and the cedar its bowers;
Where the lord of the forest, the oak, had its realm,
The ash its domain, and its kingdom the elm;
Where the pine bowed its antlers in tempests, and gave
To the ocean of leaves the wild dash of the wave;
And the mystical hemlock—the forest's high-priest—
Hung its weird, raking, top-gallant branch to the east.

And denser and deeper the solitude grew,
The underwood thickened, and drenched her with dew;
She tripped over moss-covered logs, fell, arose,
Sped, and stumbled again by the hour, till her clothes
Were rent by the branches and thorns, and her feet
Grew tender and way-worn and blistered with heat.
And on, ever on, through the forest she passed,
Her soul in her task, but each pulse beating fast,
For shadowy forms seemed to flit from the glades,
And beckon her into their limitless shades;
And mystical sounds—in the forest alone,
Ah! who has not heard them?—the voices, the moan
Or the sigh of mute nature, which sinks on the ear,
And fills us with sadness or thrills us with fear?
And who, lone and lost in the wilderness deep,
Has not felt the strange fancies, the tremors which creep
And assemble within, till the heart 'gins to fail,
The courage to flinch, and the cheeks to grow pale,
'Midst the shadows which mantle the spirit that broods
In the sombre, the deep haunted heart of the woods?

She stopped—it was noonday. The wilds she espied
Seemed solitudes measureless. "Help me!" she cried;

Her piteous lips parched with thirst, and her eyes
Strained with gazing. The sun in his infinite skies
Looked down on no creature more hapless than she,
For woman is woman where'er she may be.
For a moment she faltered, then came to her side
The heroine's spirit—the Angel of Pride.
One moment she faltered. Beware! What is this?
The coil of the serpent! the rattlesnake's hiss!
One moment, then onward. What sounds far and near?
The howl of the wolf, yet she turned not in fear,
Nor bent from her course till her eye caught a gleam,
From the woods, of a meadow through which flowed a
    stream,
Pure and sweet with the savour of leaf and of flower,
By the night-dew distilled and the soft forest shower;
Pure and cold as its spring in the rock crystalline,
Whence it gurgled and gushed 'twixt the roots of the
    pine.

And blest above bliss is the pleasure of thirst,
Where there's water to quench it; for pleasure is nursed
In the cradle of pain, and twin marvels are they
Whose interdependence is born with our clay.
Yes, blessed is water, and blessed is thirst,
Where there's water to quench it; but this is the worst
Of this life, that we reck not the blessings God sends,
Till denied them. But Laura, who felt she had friends
In Heaven, as well as on earth, knew to thank
The Giver of all things, and gratefully drank.

Once more on the pathway, through swamp and through
    mire,
Through covert and thicket, through bramble and brier,

She toiled to the highway, then over the hill,
And down the deep valley, and past the new mill,
And through the next woods, till, at sunset, she came
To the first British picket and murmured her name;
Thence, guarded by Indians, footsore and pale,
She was led to Fitzgibbon, and told him her tale.

For a moment her reason forsook her; she raved,
She laughed, and she cried—"They are saved, they are saved!"
Then her senses returned, and, with thanks loud and deep
Sounding sweetly around her, she sank into sleep.
And Bœrstler came up, but his movements were known,
His force was surrounded, his scheme was o'erthrown.
By a woman's devotion—on stone be't engraved—
The foeman was beaten, and Burlington saved.

Ah! faithful to death were our women of yore!
Have they fled with the past, to be heard of no more?
No, no! Though this laurelled one sleeps in the grave,
We have maidens as true, we have matrons as brave;
And should Canada ever be forced to the test—
To spend for our country the blood of her best—
When her sons lift the linstock and brandish the sword,
Her daughters will think of brave Laura Secord.

THE VETERAN.

J. A. Fraser.

The call "To arms!" resounded through the city broad and fair,
And volunteers in masses came, prepared to do and dare;
Young lads, whose cheeks scarce showed the down, men bearded, stout and strong,
Assembled at the first alarm, in bold undaunted throng.
"I'll volunteer!" an old man cried, "I've served the Queen before;
I fought the Russ at Inkerman, the Sepoy at Cawnpore;"
And as he stood erect and tall, with proud and flashing eye,
What though his hair were white as snow,—he could but do or die!
"You are too old," the answer was; "too old to serve her now."
Then o'er his face a wonder flashed, a scowl came on his brow,
And then a tear stole down his cheek, a sob his strong voice shook,—
"Sir, put me in a uniform, and see how old I'll look!"

IN HOSPITAL.

Annie Rothwell.

Across the glittering snow stretches the long blue
    shadows fall,
And the golden flash of the sunset creeps up on the
    white-washed wall;
If I ever reach Heaven, I wonder shall I see the sun set
    on the snows?
And if there are shadows in Heaven, will they be as blue
    as those?
Sick fancies? Maybe. Perhaps, if you'd lain here as
    long as I,
If your life was one long patience, and you knew that to
    change was to die,
You'd be thankful for even a fancy to take you out of
    your pain,
And lift you one minute,—what, crying?—there—hush,
    I won't say it again.

Too young? Ay, I'm not very old, lady; but when
    death stares you hard in the face,
There's a wonderful change comes on you: and a
    hospital ward's not the place
To grow younger, exactly. What brought me? Sit
    nearer, and bend your ear,
For this plaguy breath comes short; 'twould be hard for
    me now to join in a cheer.

We were comrades, me and Joe Linton; we shared one
    bench at school,
Together we worked in the harvest, and bathed in the
    shady pool;
He was little, and bright-eyed, and shapely, as straight
    as a balsam tree;
I'd strength, but I'd never no beauty,—folks never
    thought much of me.
To manhood we grew like brothers; then he took a
    strange fancy to roam,
And went away for a sailor, while I stayed with the old
    folks at home.
I missed him,—but 't wasn't so hard, somehow, as it
    might be to let him go;
I had learned to fear him a little—for I'd learned to love
    Mary Snow.

And I tried through the short bright summer to teach her
    to care for me;
My gentle darling, my rosebud, the sweetest girl that
    could be!
And sometimes I thought she had learned it, sometimes
    my hope was low;
But I never dared ask—an old story—but you bade me
    tell you, you know.
Well, Joe came back with the winter, and he asked me
    the question straight,—
"Have you made it out with Mary, Will? I'd as lief
    know it now as to wait."
I shook my head, for I couldn't speak, but my heart beat
    thick and fast,
As his dark eyes flashed, and—God help us both!—I
    saw the truth at last.

He was true to me, Joe. All winter he spoke to her
    never a word;
And her cheek grew pale, and the voice grew still that
    had warbled as gay as a bird;
My chance was gone, and I knew it, but a loyal heart
    had Joe,—
While I stayed he was dumb; so in spring-time 'twould
    be my turn to go.

Well, the spring-time came, and the summons; you
    remember it, lady? the call
That rang out so sharp and sudden, and struck the fire in
    us all?
I was glad, for I wanted no better than a lawful chance
    to die;
But when Joe—I thought of Mary, and I wondered, and
    asked him, why?
Then he took my hand in the old-time grip, and smiled,
    as he softly said,—
"There's One we can seek without strife, lad, and both
    win,—living or dead.
I can't let you win her alone, lad; we'll look for her side
    by side;
And whichever comes back——" I knew what he
    meant. Oh, if only I had died!

Through the hard, grand times that followed, we lived
    like brothers again;
Shared frost and fatigue and hunger, and duties of
    pleasure and pain;
Together through march and bivouac, we fared to the
    tenth of May,
And together, that Sunday morning, on the skirmish line
    we lay.

Ah! 'twas no home echo of church bells that Sabbath
    silence broke;
Command and obedience were priest and psalm, and our
    incense was rifle smoke.
But "obedience is better than sacrifice," I think I have
    heard it said;
Maybe our's will be reckoned for worship when the last
    great orders are read.

Need I tell the rest? You can guess it,—the shot and
    the swift, sharp word,
Half oath and half prayer, hurled towards me, as the
    grass where he lay was stirred:
And how I, on my knees beside him, in the waste and
    desolate place,
With his blood on my useless fingers, and his fainting
    eyes on my face,
In appeal for the help I had not, saw the desperate
    choice that must lie
Betwixt one mad effort to save him, or waiting to watch
    him die.
My arms were strong, and I clasped him,—the wide
    plain, as I raised him and ran,
Heaved to and fro around me. In that struggle of man
    for man,
My own heart choked me.... The distant lines
    seemed to mock my failing speed,
And no breath in the burden I carried gave me hope or
    strength in my need....
——The end? Well, a crack in the distance, and
    something struck my wrist,
And I shifted the weight to my shoulder that I thanked
    God the bullet had missed.

A second,—my foot slipped,—I stumbled : was it only
    over a stone ?
Ah ! this time the lead gave its message,—took tribute
    of flesh and of bone.

That's all—— I had tried and failed. When they
    found us they scarce could tell
The dead from the living. Oh, had I but died when I
    fainted and fell !
But I've lingered these long months over ('tis a weary
    time since May !)
With pain my companion in darkness, and sorrow my
    comrade by day.
They gave Joe a soldier's burial,—he has earned a
    soldier's fame ;
In the day so swiftly coming do you think I shall have
    the same ?

Had I saved him, lady, I'd have given twenty lives, nor
    counted the cost ;
But it's somewhat hard to fight one's best, yet know that
    the day is lost.
We shall know why it happens, maybe, some day, and
    perhaps we shall get our reward,
When the last retreat has been sounded, and the angels
    relieve the guard.

IN MEMORIAM.

Those killed in the North-West, 1885.

FREDERICK GEORGE SCOTT.

GROWING to full manhood now,
With the care-lines on our brow,
We, the youngest of the nations,
With no childish lamentations,
Weep, as only strong men weep,
For the noble hearts that sleep,
Pillowed where they fought and bled,
The loved and lost, our glorious dead!

Toil and sorrow come with age,
Manhood's rightful heritage;
Toil our arms more strong shall render,
Sorrow make our heart more tender,
In the heartlessness of time;
Honour lays a wreath sublime—
Deathless glory—where they bled,
Our loved and lost, our glorious dead!

Wild the prairie grasses wave
O'er each hero's new-made grave;
Time shall write such wrinkles o'er us.
But the future spreads before us
Glorious in that sunset land—
Nerving every heart and hand,
Comes a brightness none can shed,
But the dead, the glorious dead!

Lay them where they fought and fell;
Every heart shall ring their knell,
For the lessons they have taught us,
For the glory they have brought us.
Tho' our hearts are sad and bowed,
Nobleness still makes us proud—
Proud of light their names shall shed
In the roll-call of our dead !

Growing to full manhood now,
With the care-lines on our brow,
We, the youngest of the nations,
With no childish lamentations,
Weep, as only strong men weep,
For the noble hearts that sleep
Where the call of duty led,
Where the lonely prairies spread,
Where for us they fought and bled,
Our ever loved and glorious dead.

VIII.—PLACES.

VIII.—PLACES.

THE TANTRAMAR REVISITED.

Summers and summers have come, and gone with the
 flight of the swallow;
Sunshine and thunder have been, storm and winter and
 frost;
Many and many a sorrow has all but died from remem-
 brance,
Many a dream of joy fall'n in the shadow of pain.
Hands of chance and change have marred, or moulded,
 or broken,
Busy with spirit or flesh, all I most have adored;
Even the bosom of Earth is strewn with heavier
 shadows,—
Only in these green hills, aslant to the sea, no change!
Here, where the road that has climbed from the inland
 valleys and woodlands
Dips from the hill-tops down, straight to the base of the
 hills,—
Here, from my vantage-ground, I can see the scattering
 houses,

Stained with time, set warm in orchards, and meadows,
  and wheat,
Dotting the broad bright slopes outspread to southward
  and eastward,
Wind-swept all day long, blown by the south-east wind.
Skirting the sun-bright uplands stretches a riband of
  meadow,
Shorn of the labouring grass, bulwarked well from the
  sea,
Fenced on its seaward border with long clay dikes from
  the turbid
Surge and flow of the tides vexing the Westmoreland
  shores.
Yonder, towards the left, lie broad the Westmoreland
  marshes,—
Miles on miles they extend, level, and grassy, and dim,
Clear from the long red sweep of flats to the sky in the
  distance,
Save for the outlying heights, green-rampired Cumber-
  land Point;
Miles on miles outrolled, and the river-channels divide
  them,—
Miles on miles of green, barred by the hurtling gusts.

Miles on miles beyond the tawny bay is Minudie,
There are the low blue hills; villages gleam at their feet.
Nearer a white sail shines across the water, and nearer
Still are the slim grey masts of fishing boats dry on the
  flats.
Ah! how well I remember those wide red flats, above
  tide-mark,
Pale with scurf of the salt, seamed and baked in the sun!
Well I remember the piles of blocks and ropes, and the
  net-reels

Wound with the beaded nets, dripping and dark from the
    sea !
Now at this season the nets are unwound; they hang
    from the rafters
Over the fresh-stowed hay in upland barns, and the wind
Blows all day through the chinks, with the streaks of
    sunlight, and sways them
Softly at will; or they lie heaped in the gloom of a loft.

Now at this season the reels are empty and idle; I see them
Over the lines of the dikes, over the gossiping grass.
Now at this season they swing in the long strong wind,
    thro' the lonesome
Golden afternoon, shunned by the foraging gulls.
Near about sunset the crane will journey homeward
    above them;
Round them, under the moon, all the calm night long,
Winnowing soft grey wings of marsh-owls wander and
    wander,
Now to the broad lit marsh, now to the dusk of the dike.
Soon, thro' their dew-wet frames, in the live keen fresh-
    ness of morning,
Out of the teeth of the dawn blows back the awakening
    wind.
Then, as the blue day mounts, and the low-shot shafts of
    the sunlight
Glance from the tide to the shore, gossamers jewelled
    with dew
Sparkle and wave, where late sea-spoiling fathoms of
    drift-net
Myriad-meshed, uploomed sombrely over the land.

Well I remember it all. The salt raw scent of the
    margin;

While, with men at the windlass, groaned each reel, and
    the net,
Surging in ponderous lengths, uprose and coiled in its
    station ;
Then each man to his home,—well I remember it all !

Yet, as I sit and watch, this present peace of the land-
    scape,—
Stranded boats, these reels empty and idle, the hush,
One grey hawk slow-wheeling above yon cluster of hay-
    stacks,—
More than the old-time stir this stillness welcomes me
    home.

Ah, the old-time stir, how once it stung me with rapture !
Old-time sweetness, the winds freighted with honey and
    salt !
Yet will I stay my steps and not go down to the marsh-
    land,—
Muse and recall far off, rather remember than see,—
Lest, on too close sight, I miss the darling illusion,
Spy at their task even here the hands of chance and
    change.

LOW TIDE ON GRAND-PRÉ.

Bliss Carman.

The sun goes down, and over all
    These barren reaches by the tide
Such unelusive glories fall,
    I almost dream they yet will bide
    Until the coming of the tide.

And yet I know that not for us,
　By any ecstasy of dream,
He lingers to keep luminous
　A little while the grievous stream,
　Which frets, uncomforted of dream,—

A grievous stream, that to and fro
　Athrough the fields of Acadie
Goes wandering, as if to know
　Why one beloved face should be
　So long from home and Acadie!

Was it a year or lives ago
　We took the grasses in our hands,
And caught the summer flying low
　Over the waving meadow lands,
　And held it there between our hands?

The while the river at our feet—
　A drowsy inland meadow stream—
At set of sun the after-heat
　Made running gold, and in the gleam
　We freed our birch upon the stream.

There down along the elms at dusk
　We lifted dripping blade to drift,
Through twilight scented fine like musk,
　Where night and gloom awhile uplift,
　Nor sunder soul and soul adrift.

And that we took into our hands—
  Spirit of life or subtler thing—
Breathed on us there, and loosed the bands
  Of death, and taught us, whispering,
  The secret of some wonder-thing.

Then all your face grew light, and seemed
  To hold the shadow of the sun;
The evening faltered, and I deemed
  That time was ripe, and years had done
  Their wheeling underneath the sun.

So all desire and all regret,
  And fear and memory, were naught;
One to remember or forget
  The keen delight our hands had caught;
  Morrow and yesterday were naught!

The night has fallen, and the tide . . .
  Now and again comes drifting home,
Across these aching barrens wide,
  A sigh like driven wind or foam:
  In grief the flood is bursting home!

THE INDIAN NAMES OF ACADIA.

Attributed to De Mille.

The memory of the Red Man,
  How can it pass away,
While his names of music linger
  On each mount and stream and bay?
While *Musquodobit's* waters
  Roll sparkling to the main;
While falls the laughing sunbeam
  On *Chegogin's* fields of grain.

While floats our country's banner
  O'er *Chebucto's* glorious wave;
And the frowning cliffs of *Scaterie*
  The trembling surges brave;
While breezy *Aspotogon*
  Lifts high its summit blue,
And sparkles on its winding way
  The gentle *Sissibou*.

While *Escasoni's* fountains
  Pour down their crystal tide;
While *Inganish's* mountains
  Lift high their forms of pride;
Or while on *Mabou's* river
  The boatman plies his oar;
Or the billows burst in thunder
  On *Chickaben's* rock-girt shore.

The memory of the Red Man,
  It lingers like a spell
On many a storm-swept headland,
  On many a leafy dell;
Where *Tusket's* thousand islets,
  Like emeralds, stud the deep;
Where *Blomidon*, a sentry grim,
  His endless watch doth keep.

It dwells round *Catalon's* blue lake,
  'Mid leafy forests hid,—
Round fair *Discourse*, and the rushing tides
  Of the turbid *Pisiquid*.
And it lends, *Chebogue*, a touching grace
  To thy softly flowing river,
As we sadly think of the gentle race
  That has passed away for ever.

ON LEAVING THE COAST OF NOVA SCOTIA.

George Frederick Cameron.

I STAND alone at midnight on the deck,
And watch with eager eye the sinking shore
Which I may view, it may be, nevermore;
For there is tempest, battle, fire, and wreck,
And Ocean hath her share of each of these,—
Attest it, thousand rotten argosies,
Wealth-laden, sunken in the southern seas!

And who can say that evermore these feet
　Shall tread thy soil, Acadia? Who can say
That evermore this heart of mine shall greet
The loved to whom it sighs adieu to-day?
Our sail is set for countries far away;
Our sail is set, and now is no retreat,
　Though Ocean should but lure, like Beauty,
　　　to betray!

THE FAIRIES IN PRINCE EDWARD ISLAND.

(*From "The Emigration of the Fairies."*)

JOHN HUNTER-DUVAR.

FIRST halt. They heard within a sugar patch
　The rhyming tic-a-tac of axes chopping,
So scouts were sent ahead to try to catch
　A glimpse of whom or what 'twas caused the lopping,
And bring back a description of the natives—
If they were cannibals or friends, or caitiffs.

The scouts returned and said where they had stole,
　They'd seen a score or so of stalwart creatures
In flannel shirts, not smock-frocks; on the whole
　They rather liked their friendly bearded features,
And that the first glance of these live Canadians
Impressed them favourably—(they were Acadians).

Then onward.   Sudden on the horizon came
   A burst of blaze like to a town on fire,
While smoke in columns and fierce tongues of flame
   Rose grandly heavenwards, high and ever higher—
They were so scared they went by with a rush,
And did not know 'twas choppers burning brush.

With feelings as on field of Waterloo,
   They came upon a space of blackened stumps;
"Alas!" cried they, "here greenwood temples grew,
   And columns, ruined now, have stood in clumps."
They thought that war had here wiped out a nation
And left this ghastly scene of desolation.

They reached a scaffold frame beside a weir
   With criss-cross beams, and rafters gaunt and slewed,
And in it agonising screams could hear,
   And saw a whirling fiend devouring wood—
It was a sawmill, and, too scared for speech,
They skirred away beyond the monster's reach.

It pleased them much to see the birds about,
   And one boy cried, "A robin! big as thrush!
Ma, can that be Cock Robin grown so stout?"
   Whereon his mother, with her thoughts a-rush
With English memories, said (and checked a sob in),
"My dear, that is a fowl and not a robin."

They saw woodpeckers hanging by the toes,
   Bluejay they thought was a professional beauty;
They looked for rooks but only lit on crows,
   Whose only link with crows, is both are sooty;
And as to linnets, finches, and those others,
They looked on them in light of little brothers.

A number of strange other things they noted
   As quite unlike what they had seen at home,
To all of which they curiously devoted
   Attention, as a gentle hill they clomb,
Where on them burst a true colonial scene
Of wood and meadow land of living green.

THE VALE OF THE GASPEREAU.

(From " Gaspereau.")

ARTHUR JOHN LOCKHART.

WOE fell on you, ye genial race,
   Ye exiled sons of lily France!
This is no more your dwelling-place,—
   Ye live in music and romance;
But oft as purple even-tide
   Bathes all these hills in fire and dew,
Some wanderer by the river-side
   Shall drop a tear and dream of you.

The Vale still rings with childhood's song,
   Amid its yellowing sea of flowers,
While days of summer glide along
   On wings of light through all your bowers.
Here are the trees ye planted, here
   The remnants of your broken homes;
But to old graves from year to year,
   No ghostly mourner ever comes.

THE ISLE OF DEMONS.

(From " Marguerite.")

GEORGE MARTIN.

TOGETHER o'er the mystic Isle
We wandered many a sinuous mile.
'Twas midway in the month of June,
And rivulets with lisping rune,
And bowering trees of tender green,
And flowering shrubs their trunks between,
Enticed our steps till gloaming grey
Upon the pathless forest lay.
Think not I journeyed void of fear;
   Sir Roberval's hot malediction,
Like hurtling thunder, sounded near;
Our steps the envious demons haunted,
   And peeped, or seemed to peep and leer,
   From rocky clefts and caverns drear.
But still, defiantly, undaunted,
Eugene averred it had been held
By wise philosophers of eld
That all such sights and sounds are mere
Fantastic tricks of eye and ear,
   And only meet for tales of fiction.
"Heed not," he said, "the vicious threat,
   'Twas but a ruffian's empty talk,
The which I pray thou may'st forget
   And half his evil purpose baulk."
A silent doubt and grateful kiss
Was all I could oppose to this.

But firmer grew my steps.   The air
    Was laden with delicious balm;
Rich exhalations everywhere,
    From pine and spruce and cedar grove,
And over all a dreamy calm,
    An affluence of brooding love,
A palpable, beneficent
Sufficiency of blest content.

Amid the hours, in restful pause
    We loitered on the moss-clad rocks,
And listened to the sober caws
    Of lonely rooks, and watched thick flocks
Of pigeons passing overhead;
Or where the scarlet grosbeak sped,
    A wingéd fire, through clumps of pine
Sent chasing looks of joy and wonder.
    Blue violets and celandine,
And modest ferns that glanced from under
Grey-hooded boulders, seemed to say—
"O, tarry, gentle folk; O, stay,
    For we are lonely in this wood,
And sigh for human sympathy
    To cheer our days of solitude."

. . . .

The great rude world was far away,
And like a troubled vision lay
Outside our thoughts; its cold deceits,
The babble of its noisy streets,
And all the selfish rivalry
That courts and castles propagate

Were alien to our new estate.—
A fragment of propitious sky,
Whereon a puff of cloud might lie,
Through verdured boughs o'er-arching seen,
And glimpses of the sea between
Far stretches of majestic trees,
Such peaceful sanctities as these
Were our abiding joyance now.

Cheerily, and with lifted brow,
Eugene led on, where tamaracs grew,
And where tall elms their shadows threw
Athwart a little glen, wherein
A virgin brook seemed glad to win
The pressure of our thirsty lips.
   Pleasant it was to linger there
And cool our fevered finger-tips
   In that pellucid stream, and share
The solace of the ocean breeze.
   For summer heats were now aglow,
The fox sat down and took his ease,
   The hare moved purposeless and slow
But louder rang the bluejay's scream,
   The woodpeck tapped the naked tree,
   Nor ceased the simple chicadee
To twitter in the noonday beam.—
My lover, wheresoe'er we strayed,
   Made search in every charmed nook,
   And angled in the winding brook
For all sweet flowers that love the shade,
To twine for me a bridal braid.
Pale yellow lilies, nursed by rocks
Rifted and scarred by lightning shocks,
Or earthquake; river buds and pinks,

And modest snow-drops, pearly white,
And lilies of the vale, unite
Their beauty in close-loving links
Around a scented woodbine fair
To coronate my dark brown hair.
The fragile fern and clover sweet
On that enchanted circlet meet;
Young roses lent their blushing hues;
Nor could the cedar leaf refuse
With helmet flowers to intertwine
Its glossy amplitude divine.—
Emerging from that solemn wood,
High on a rocky cliff we stood
At set of sun; far, far away
The splendours of departing day
Upon the barren ocean lay.—
There on that lone sea-beaten height,
Investured in a golden light,
Eugene, with looks half sad, whole sweet,
Upon my brow the garland set,
At once a chaplet and aigrette,
And said "Be crowned, my Marguerite!"

Was it sick fancy, sore misled,
That to my shuddering spirit said?—
"Those sounds that shake the midnight air,
Are threats of Shapes that will not spare
Your trespass on their fief accurst."
"Hush, hush, my love," Eugene would say,
"That cry which o'er our cabin burst
Came from the owls, perched royally
Among the pine-tops; you but heard
The language of some beast or bird;
The mooing of a mother bear,

An hungered in her frozen lair;
The laugh and mooing of the loon
That welcometh the rising moon.
The howling of the wolves you hear,
In chase of some unhappy deer,
Impeded in its desperate flight
   By deep and thickly crusted snows,
   O'er which its lighter-footed foes
Pursue like shadows of the night.
That lengthened groan, that fearful shriek,
Was but the grinding stress and creak
Of aged trees; they seem to feel
The wrench of storms, and make appeal
For mercy; in their ducts and cells
The sap, which is their life-blood, swells
When frosts prevail, and bursts asunder
With sharp report its prison walls."

  .   .   .   .   .   .

The double darkness walled us in,
   The blackness of the storm and night,
And still he came not! O, what sin,
   What blasphemy against the light
Of Heaven had my soul committed?
   Never before had eventide
   Once found him absent from my side.
Eugene came not! deceived, outwitted,
   Sore tempest-tossed and lured astray
By demons, when the night-owl flitted
   Across his face at close of day,
Groping for home, exhausted, faint,
No angel near, no pitying saint
   To aid his steps and point the way!

From ebb of day till noon of night,
And onward till return of light,
The signal horn, Nanette and I,
Alternate blew; but for reply
The wind's unprecedented roar,
And ocean thundering round the shore
Our labour mocked; and other sounds,
Nor of the land, nor sea, nor sky,
Our ears profaned; the unleashed hounds
Of spleenful hell were all abroad,
And round our snow-bound cabin trod,
And stormed on clashing wings aloof,
And stamped upon the yielding roof,
And all our lamentation jeered.
Down the wide chimney-gorge they peered
   With great green eye-balls fringed with
      flame;—
The holy cross I kissed and reared,
   And in sweet Mary's blessed name,
Who erst had buoyed my sinking heart,
Conjured the foul-faced fiends depart.
Their shriekings made a storm more loud
Than that before whose fury bowed
The hundred-ringéd oaken trees;
More fearful, more appalling these
Than thunder from the thunder-cloud.

———

SAGUENAY.

(From the French of Fréchette.)

J. D. Edgar.

The forest has spells to enchant me,
    The mountain has power to enthrall;
Yet the grace of a wayside blossom
    Can stir my heart deeper than all.

O towering steeps, that are mirrored
    On Saguenay's darkening breast!
O grim rocky heights, sternly frowning,
    The thunders have smitten your crest!

O sentinels, piercing the cloudland,
    Stand forth in stupendous array!
My brow, by your shadows enshrouded,
    Is humbled before you to-day.

But, peaks that are gilded by Heaven,
    Defiant you stand in your pride!
From glories too distant, above me,
    I turn to the friend by my side.

QUEBEC.

Charles Sangster.

Quebec! how regally it crowns the height,
Like a tanned giant on a solid throne!
Unmindful of the sanguinary fight,
The roar of cannon mingling with the moan
Of mutilated soldiers years agone,
That gave the place a glory and a name
Among the nations. France was heard to groan;
England rejoiced, but checked the proud acclaim,—
A brave young chief had fall'n to vindicate her fame.

Wolfe and Montcalm! two nobler names ne'er graced
The page of history, or the hostile plain;
No braver souls the storm of battle faced,
Regardless of the danger or the pain.
They passed unto their rest without a stain
Upon their nature or their generous hearts.
One graceful column to the noble twain
Speaks of a nation's gratitude, and starts
The tear that Valour claims and Feeling's self imparts.

MONTREAL.

William M'Lennan.

Sprung from the hope of noble hearts,
    Brought into being through sacrifice
Of men and women who played their parts,
    And counted not their lives as the price.
She has grown in her strength like a Northern Queen,
    'Neath her crown of light and her robe of snow,
And stands in her beauty fair, between
    The Royal Mount and the River below.

Changing its hue with the changing skies,
    The river flows in its beauty rare;
While across the plain eternal, rise
    Boucherville, Rougemont, and St. Hilaire.
Far to the westward lies Lachine,
    Gate of the Orient long ago,
When the virgin forest swept between
    The Royal Mount and the River below.

With its convent buildings low and white
    Nun's Island lies, half wood, half plain;
While abreast of the city, green and bright
    Springs the wooded crest of St. Helene.
In the east the shimmer of waves is seen,
    Where the River spreads in its onward flow
From the Royal City that lies between
    The Royal Mount and the River below.

THE ST. LAWRENCE.

K. L. JONES.

SWIFT from Ontario's side,
   Hating the lake's cold embraces,
Laughing, the blue waters glide
   Into far pleasanter places;
Threading the maze of the isles,
   Shimmering, shivering ever,
Wearing a wreathlet of smiles,
   Rolls the great river;

Trending through darkness and day,
   Fondling the dawning and gloaming;
Tossing huge billows and spray,
   High, when the Storm King is roaming;
Mirroring chalet-crowned rocks,
   Fern leaves, long grasses, and clover,
Wild fowls in myriad flocks
   As they fly over;

Sleeping in lily-starred bays;
   Rushing through factory races,
Where o'er the looms ever gaze
   Hundreds of bloom-bereft faces;
Wid'ning to lakelets and meres,
   Wildly o'er cascades careering,
Sweeping by bridges and piers,
   Ocean-ward bearing;

Chafing the Laurentide shores,—
    Cliffs frowning over, and under
Hurtling the dark waters roar
    As if they would tear them asunder,—
Past the grim fortress and plain
    Linked with brave Wolfe and his story,
Pealing in pæan's refrain
    Canada's glory;

Stretching her arms to the world,
    Wide, as a maid to her lover;
Coyly, with banners unfurled,
    Welcoming argosies over;
Wearied, her life's journey done,
    Grateful to God, the life-giver,
Her goal on the ocean's breast won,
    Rests the great river.

NIGHT IN THE THOUSAND ISLES.

CHARLES SANGSTER.

AND now 'tis night. A myriad stars have come
To cheer the earth and sentinel the skies.
The full-orbed moon irradiates the gloom,
And fills the air with light. Each islet lies
Immersed in shadow, soft as thy dark eyes;
Swift through the sinuous path our vessel glides,
Now hidden by the massive promontories,
Anon the bubbling silver from its sides
Spurning, like a wild-bird whose home is on the tides.

Here Nature holds her Carnival of Isles.
Steeped in warm sunlight all the merry day,
Each nodding tree and floating greenwood smiles,
And moss-crowned monsters move in grim array;
All night the Fisher spears his finny prey;
The piney flambeaux reddening the deep,
Past the dim shores, or up some mimic bay;
Like grotesque banditti they boldly sweep
Upon the startled prey, and stab them while they sleep.

Many a tale of legendary lore
Is told of these romantic Isles.   The feet
Of the Red Man have pressed each wave-zoned shore,
And many an eye of beauty oft did greet
The painted warriors and their birchen fleet,
As they returned with trophies of the slain.
That race has passed away; their fair retreat
In its primeval loneness smiles again,
Save where some vessel snaps the isle-enwoven chain;

Save where the echo of the huntsman's gun
Startles the wild duck from some shallow nook,
Or the swift hounds' deep baying, as they run,
Rouses the lounging student from his book;
Or where, assembled by some sedgy brook,
A picnic party, resting in the shade,
Spring pleasedly to their feet, to catch a look
At the strong steamer, through the watery glade
Ploughing, like a huge serpent from its ambuscade.

OTTAWA.

Before Dawn.

Duncan Campbell Scott.

The stars are stars of morn; a keen wind wakes
The birches on the slope; the distant hills
Rise in the vacant North; the Chaudière fills
The calm with its hushed roar; the river takes
An unquiet rest, and a bird stirs, and shakes
The morn with music; a snatch of singing thrills
From the river; and the air clings and chills.
Fair, in the South, fair as a shrine that makes
The wonder of a dream, imperious towers
Pierce and possess the sky, guarding the halls
Where our young strength is welded strenuously;
While in the East, the star of morning dowers
The land with a large tremulous light, that falls
A pledge and presage of our destiny.

AT THE FERRY.

E. Pauline Johnson.

We are waiting in the nightfall by the river's placid rim,
Summer silence all about us, save where swallows' pinions skim
The still grey waters sharply, and the widening circles reach,
With faintest, stillest music, the white gravel on the beach.

The sun has set long, long ago. Against the pearly sky
Elm branches lift their etching up in arches slight and high.
Behind us stands the forest, with its black and lonely pines;
Before us, like a silver thread, the old Grand River winds.
Far down its banks the village lights are creeping one by one;
Far up above, with holy torch, the evening star looks down.

Amid the listening stillness, you and I have silent grown,
Waiting for the river ferry,—waiting in the dusk alone.
At last we hear a velvet step, sweet silence reigns no more;
'Tis a barefoot, sunburnt little boy upon the other shore.
Far thro' the waning twilight we can see him quickly kneel
To lift the heavy chain, then turn the rusty old cog-wheel;
And the water-logged old ferry-boat moves slowly from the brink,
Breaking all the star's reflections with the waves that rise and sink;
While the water dripping gently from the rising, falling chains,
Is the only interruption to the quiet that remains
To lull us into golden dreams, to charm our cares away
With its Lethean waters flowing 'neath the bridge of yesterday.
Oh! the day was calm and tender, but the night is calmer still,
As we go aboard the ferry, where we stand and dream, until
We cross the sleeping river, with its restful whisperings,
And peace falls, like a feather from some passing angel's wings.

NIAGARA.

From "The U. E."

WILLIAM KIRBY.

Now sailed the cloudless moon through seas of light
And dimmed the sleepless stars that watch the night,
As swiftly turning from the sandy lane
The riders crossed a spacious rolling plain,
Hedged by the lofty screen of dusky woods
That hide Niagara's deep-embedded floods.
White clouds of mist rolled upward on the breeze,
Swept o'er the brink, and dripped among the trees;
While earth and air, in tremor all around,
Shook in dread cadence to the rumbling sound
That rises up from Nature's troubled womb,
With war unbroken till the day of doom.
They hurried on; the woody veil withdrew,
The wondrous vision swept full into view;
Niagara's twin-born cataracts descend,
And eye and ear with their contention rend.
A spot of chaos, from Creation's day
Left unsubdued, to show the world alway
What was the earth ere God's commandment ran
That light should be, and order first began.

The riders halt, and for a moment stay,
While Ranger John half chid the brief delay.
Though often seen before, with fresh desire
The glorious vision still they each admire.
Spread o'er the south, a furious tumbling sea
Rolls down the steep incline, as wild and free

As when with tossing heads and flowing manes
The desert steeds in herds sweep o'er the plains,—
As in th' Olympic Stadium's final round
The chariot wheels revolve with thundering sound,
While veiled in clouds of dust the champions fly,
And shouts and turmoil shake the earth and sky!

Thus down the rocky rapids, side by side,
A thousand foaming currents madly ride;
Now mingling, now dividing, each and all
Still swifter hurry to the final goal.
There, waves that washed Superior's rocky strand,
And rolled transparent o'er her silver sand,
So pure and limpid, that they seemed to bear
The bark canoe afloat in very air,
Now, lashed to madness, o'er the rapids ran,
Yoked to the darker waves of Michigan;
St. Clair's shoal streams, and Huron's haunted floods
That tumbled round the Manitoulin woods,
And fretful Erie's waters, in dismay
Sweep white with terror down the shelvy way.

In vain, Goat Island, dank, and grim with scars
Of an eternity of watery wars,
With stony shoulder stems the rushing tides
That right and left his dripping shore divides.
They 'scape his grasp, and o'er the jutting brink
Sheer down on either hand impetuous sink;
The vail of waters rending, as they go
'Mid storms of mist into the gulf below,
Where, face to face, the sundered torrents pour
In rival cataracts, with deafening roar,
Mingle their sprays, and with their mighty war
Shake earth's deep centre with eternal jar.

That dread abyss! What mortal tongue may tell
The seething horrors of its watery hell!
Where, pent in craggy walls that gird the deep,
Imprisoned tempests howl, and madly sweep
The tortured floods, drifting from side to side
In furious vortices, that circling ride
Around the deep arena; or, set free
From depths unfathomed, bursts a boiling sea
In showers of mist and spray, that leap and bound
Against the dripping rocks; while loud resound
Ten thousand thunders, that as one conspire
To strike the deepest note of Nature's lyre.

THE HEART OF THE LAKES.

William Wilfred Campbell.

There are crags that loom like spectres
  Half under the sun and the mist,
There are beaches that gleam and glisten,
There are ears that open to listen,
  And lips held up to be kissed.

There are miles and miles of waters
  That throb like a woman's breast,
With a glad harmonious motion,
  Like happiness caught at rest;
As if a heart beat under
  In love with its own glad rest,
Beating and beating for ever
  Outward to east and to west.

There are forests that kneel for ever,
   Robed in the dreamiest haze
That God sends down in the Summer
   To mantle the gold of its days;
Kneeling and leaning for ever
   In winding and sinuous bays.

There are birds that like smoke-drift hover
   With a strange and bodeful cry,
Into the dream and the distance
   Of the marshes that southward lie
With their lonely lagoons and rivers
   Far under the reeling sky.

MANITOU.

WILLIAM WILFRED CAMPBELL.

[The island of the Manitou, the largest island in Lake Huron, believed by the Indians to be sacred to Manitou when he makes his abode on earth.]

GIRDLED by Huron's throbbing and thunder,
   Out on the drift and rift of its blue;
Walled by mists from the world asunder,
Far from all hate and passion and wonder,
   Lieth the isle of the Manitou.

Here, where the surfs of the great Lake trample,
   Thundering time-worn caverns through,
Beating on rock-coasts aged and ample,
Reareth the Manitou's mist-walled temple,
   Floored with forest and roofed with blue.

Grey crag-battlements, seared and broken,
    Keep these passes for ages to come ;
Never a watchword here is spoken,
Never a single sign or token,
    From hands that are motionless, lips that are dumb.

Only the sun-god rideth over,
    Marking the seasons with track of flame ;
Only the wild-fowl float and hover,—
Flocks of clouds, whose white wings cover
    Spaces on spaces without a name.

Stretches of marsh and wild lake-meadow,
    Beaches that bend to the edge of the world ;
Morn and even, suntime and shadow ;
Wild flame of sunset over far meadow,
    Fleets of white vapours sun-kissed and furled

Year by year the ages onward
    Drift, but it lieth out here alone ;
Earthward the mists, and the earth-mists sunward ;
Starward the days, and the nights bloom dawnward ;
    Whisper the forests, the beaches make moan.

Far from the world, and its passions fleeting,
    Neath quiet of noonday and stillness of star,
Shore unto shore each sendeth greeting,
Where the only woe is the surf's wild beating
    That throbs from the maddened lake afar.

THE LAST BISON.
Charles Mair.

Eight years have fled since, in the wilderness,
I drew the rein to rest my comrade there,—
My supple, clean-limbed pony of the plains.
He was a runner of pure Indian blood,
Yet in his eye still gleamed the desert's fire,
And form and action both bespoke the Barb.
A wondrous creature is the Indian's horse;
Degenerate now, but from the "Centaur" drawn,—
The furious Fifty which dissolved with fear
Montezuma's plumed Children of the Sun,
And shared rough Cortez in his realm of gold!

A gentle vale, with rippling aspens clad,
Yet open to the breeze, invited rest.
So there I lay, and watched the sun's fierce beams
Reverberate in wreathed ethereal flame;
Or gazed upon the leaves which buzzed o'erhead,
Like tiny wings in simulated flight.
Within the vale a lakelet, lashed with flowers,
Lay like a liquid eye among the hills,
Revealing in its depths the fulgent light
Of snowy cloudland and cerulean skies.
And rising, falling, fading far around,
The homeless and unfurrowed prairies spread
In solitude and idleness eterne.
And all was silence, save the rustling leaf,
The gadding insect, or the grebe's lone cry;
Or where Saskatchewan, with turbid moan,
Deep-sunken in the plain, his torrent poured.
Here loneliness possessed her realm supreme—
Her prairies all about her, undeflowered,
Pulsing beneath the summer sun, and sweet

With virgin air and waters undefiled.
Inviolate still ! Bright solitudes with power
To charm the spirit, bruised, where ways are foul,
Into forgetfulness of chuckling wrong,
And all the weary clangour of the world.

Yet Sorrow, too, had here its kindred place,
As o'er my spirit swept the sense of change.
Here sympathy could sigh o'er man's decay;
For here, but yesterday, the warrior dwelt
Whose faded nation had for ages held,
In fealty to Nature, these domains.
Around me were the relics of his race,—
The grassy circlets where his village stood,
Well ruled by custom's immemorial law.
Along these slopes his happy offspring roved
In days gone by, and dusky mothers plied
Their summer tasks, or loitered in the shade.
Here the magician howled his demons up;
And here the lodge of council had its seat,
Once resonant with oratory wild.
All vanished ! perished in the swelling sea
And stayless tide of an encroaching power,
Whose civil fiat, man-devouring still,
Will leave at last no wilding on the earth
To wonder at or love.

               With them had fled
The bison,—breed which overflowed the plains,
And, undiminished, fed uncounted tribes.
Its vestiges were here,—its wallows, paths,
And skulls and shining ribs and vertebræ;
Grey bones of monarchs, from the herds perchance
Descended, by De Vaca first beheld,
Or Coronado, in mad quest of gold.

Here hosts had had their home; here had they roamed,
Endless and infinite,—vast herds which seemed
Exhaustless as the sea.   All vanished now !
Of that wild tumult not a hoof remained
To scour the countless paths where myriads trod.

Long had I lain, 'twixt dreams and waking, thus :
Musing on change and mutability,
And endless evanescence, when a burst
Of sudden roaring filled the vale with sound.
Perplexed and startled, to my feet I sprang,
And in amazement from my covert gazed,
For presently into the valley came
A mighty bison, which with stately tread
And gleaming eyes descended to the shore !
Spell-bound I stood.   Was this a living form,
Or but an image by the fancy drawn ?
But no,—he breathed! and from a wound blood flowed
And trickled with the frothing from his lips.
Uneasily he gazed, yet saw me not,
Haply concealed; then, with a roar so loud
That all the echoes rent their valley-horns,
He stood and listened; but no voice replied !
Deeply he drank, then lashed his quivering flanks,
And roared again, and hearkened, but no sound,
No tongue congenial answered to his call,—
He was the last survivor of his clan !

Huge was his frame ! emasculate, so grown
To that enormous bulk whose presence filled
The very vale with awe.   His shining horns
Gleamed black amidst his fell of floating hair;
His neck and shoulders, of the lion's build,
Were framed to toss the world !   Now stood he there,

And stared, with head uplifted, at the skies,
Slow-yielding to his deep and mortal wound.
He seemed to pour his mighty spirit out
As thus he gazed, till my own spirit burned,
And teeming fancy, charmed and overwrought
By all the wildering glamour of the scene,
Gave to that glorious altitude a voice,
And, rapt, endowed the noble beast with song.

THE SONG.

Hear me, ye smokeless skies and grass green earth,
    Since by your sufferance still I breathe and live!
Through you fond Nature gave me birth
    And food and freedom,—all she had to give.
Enough! I grew, and with my kindred ranged
Their realm stupendous, changeless, and unchanged,
    Save by the toll of nations primitive,
Who throve on us, and loved our life-stream's roar,
And lived beside its wave, and camped upon its shore.

They loved us, but they wasted not. They slew,
    With pious hand, but for their daily need;
Not wantonly, but as the due
    Of stern necessity which Life doth breed.
Yea, even as earth gave us its herbage meet,
So yielded we, in turn, our substance sweet
    To quit the claims of hunger, not of greed.
So stood it with us, that what either did
Could not be on the earth foregone, nor Heaven forbid.

And so companioned in the blameless strife
    Enjoined upon all creatures, small and great,
Our ways were venial, and our life
    Ended in fair fulfilment of our fate.

No gold to them by sordid hands were passed;
No greedy herdsman housed us from the blast.
   Ours was the liberty of regions rife,
In winter's snow, in summer's fruits and flowers,—
Ours were the virgin prairies, and their rapture ours!

So fared it with us both; yea, thus it stood
   In all our wanderings from place to place,
Until the red man mixed his blood
   With paler currents. Then arose a race—
The reckless hunters of the plains—who vied
In wanton slaughter for the tongue and hide,
   To satisfy vain ends and longings base.
This grew; and yet we flourished, and our name
Prospered upon the earth, until the pale-faced con-
    course came.

Then fell a double terror on the plains,
   The swift inspreading of destruction dire,—
Strange men, who ravaged our domains
   On every hand, and ringed us round with fire;
Pale enemies, who slew with equal mirth
The harmless or the hurtful things of earth,
   In dead fruition of their mad desire;
The ministers of mischief and of might,
Who yearn for havoc as the world's supreme delight.

So waned the myriads, which had waxed before
   When subject to the simple needs of men.
As yields to eating seas the shore,
   So yielded our vast multitude; and then—
It scattered! Meagre bands, in wild dismay,
Were parted, and for shelter fled away
   To barren wastes, to mountain gorge and glen;
A respite brief from stern pursuit and care,
For still the spoiler sought, and still he slew us there.

Hear me, thou grass-green earth, ye smokeless skies,
  Since by your sufferance still I breathe and live!
The charity which man denies
  Ye still would tender to the fugitive!
I feel your mercy in my veins; at length
My heart revives, and strengthens with your strength.
  Too late, too late, the courage ye would give!
Nought can avail these wounds, this failing breath,
This frame which feels, at last, the wily touch of death.

Here must the last of all his kindred fall;
  Yet, 'midst these gathering shadows, ere I die,—
Responsive to an inward call,—
  My spirit fain would rise and prophesy.
I see our spoilers build their cities great
Upon our plains,—I see their rich estate;
  The centuries in dim procession fly!
Long ages roll, and then at length is bared
The time when they who spared not are no longer
     spared.

Once more my vision sweeps the prairies wide:
  But now, no peopled cities greet the sight,—
All perished now, their pomp and pride;
  In solitude the wild wind takes delight.
Nought but the vacant wilderness is seen,
And grassy mounds where cities once had been:
  The earth smiles as of yore, the skies are bright,
Wild cattle graze and bellow on the plain,
And savage nations roam o'er native wilds again!

  The burden ceased: and now, with head bowed down
  The bison smelt, then grinned into the air.
  An awful anguish seized his giant frame,
  Cold shudderings and indrawn gaspings deep,—

The spasms of illimitable pain.
One stride he took, and sank upon his knees,
Glared stern defiance where I stood revealed,
Then swayed to earth, and, with convulsive groan,
Turned heavily upon his side, and died.

A PRAIRIE YEAR.
From "Eos: A Prairie Dream."
NICHOLAS FLOOD DAVIN.

THE depths of infinite shade,
 The soft green dusk of the glade,
With fiery fingers the frost had fret,
 And dyed a myriad hue,
Making of forests temples of golden aisles;
 The swooning rose forgot to bloom;
 In fragrant graves slept violets blue;
 And earlier shook her locks of jet
Night, with her subtle shadowy wiles,—
 Night, with her starry gloom,—
Before, like suns which could not set,
 Your eyes shone clear on mine,
Flushing the heart with feelings high,
Touching all life, as thrills the sky
When over cloudy pavements thunders rumble
  and roll;
 Then flamed the faltering blood like wine,
  And overflowed the soul.

Through wintry weeks, the sun above
 Oceaned in blue, the frost below;
Through blustry hours, when fiercely drove
 Winds razor-armed the drifting snow,

And peeled the face and pinched the ear,
And hurled the avalanche of fear
From roof-tops on the mufflered crowd;
　　The air one blinding cloud;—
Through many a brisk and bracing day,
　　The sky wide summer as in June,
　　The joyous sleigh-bells' ringing tune
More blithe than aught musicians play;
　　The pure snow gleaming white;
　　Men's eyes fulfilled of finer light,
Of finer tints the women's hair;
　　Their cheeks aglow, and full and pink;
　　The skaters sweeping through the rink,
Like swallows through the air:
We talked and walked, and laughed and dreamed,
　　And now snow-wreaths, auroral rays,
　　The winter moon, day's blinding blaze,
　　The merry bells, the skaters' grace,
　　Recall thy laugh, recall thy face
As dazzling as it earliest beamed!

Love stirred in the frozen branches,
　　And straight the world was crown'd with green;
And as a shipwright his trim craft launches,
Each bud put forth in a night its might,
　　And the trees stood proud in summer sheen,
　　Their foliage dense a grateful screen
'Gainst the bold bright heat and the full fierce light.
Like cathedral windows the gardens glowed;
　　Mirrors of light the broad lakes gleamed;
His cunning in song the robin showed,
　　And the shore-lark swung on a branch and dreamed;
And boats were gliding, lover-laden,

Over lakes and streams that will yet be known,
The boy in flannel, the blooming maiden
   In muslin white with a ribbon zone.
The chestnuts fell. From their dull green sheaths
   With satin-white linings the nuts burst free;
And as sundown came, bright hazy wreaths
   The spirit of eve hung from tree to tree.
The weeks rolled on, the lush green fields
   Became billowy breadths of golden grain,
And all roots and fruits the kind earth yields
   Were piled on the labouring wain.—
And you were by the cliff-barred white-crested sea,
   And I where the delicate pink of the prairie rose
     Amid rich coarse grasses hides;
Where the sunset's boisterous pageantry,
   And the mornings the tenderest tints disclose,
Where far from the shade and shelter of wood
The prairie hen rears her speckled brood,
     And the prairie wolf abides;
And lonely memory, searching through,
   Found no such stars in the orbèd past,
As the glad first greeting 'twixt me and you,
   And the sad, mad meeting which was our last.

THE LEGEND OF THUNDER.

H. R. A. POCOCK.

Note by Walpole Roland, Esq., C.E., with which this ballad is headed in his recent work, "Algoma West":—"Among the most popular traditions touching the origin of this suggestive title, 'Thunder Cape,' is the following as related in the Otchipiway, by 'Weisaw,' and very freely translated by a friend of the writer's:—'Long years ago, while my great-great-grandfather, then a young brave, was returning with a war-party from a bloody encounter with our foes (the Sioux) near Dog Mountain, a place twenty-five miles north-west of the Kaministiquia River, their attention was suddenly arrested by loud and prolonged reverberations, accompanied by vivid flashes of lightning. Ascending the heights overlooking the Kitchee Gamee (Lake Superior), an appalling sight met their gaze. Far out in the bay towards the east, where the "Sleeping Giant" Nanibijou usually reclined on his fleecy couch, all appeared in flames, while at intervals great pinnacles or shafts of flame and black clouds were driven upwards with terrible fury. . . . Arriving at the mouth of the Kaministiquia River, they were told of the fate of two hunters from a distant tribe who, regardless of repeated warnings, provoked the fiery spirit of the great "Thunder Eagle" by ascending its home in the cloud-capped cliff, and perished in the vain attempt to bring down a great medicine. Previous to the advent of the white man our storms were grander and more frequent, and only upon rare occasions indeed could a view from a distance be obtained of the Cape or Nanibijou.'"

BEHOLD the gentle waters lap against the Giant's side,
The playful whispers of the winds that by his slumber glide,
The warm sun bending o'er his sleep, the breathing of the sea,
The cool grey shadows nestled down beneath each fragrant tree.
The Monarch of this sombre land, he dwells in clouded state
Beside the portals of the East, where yonder mighty gate
At morning sunders his broad leaves to let the daylight in,
When Night must quit the Giant's throne, and conqu'ring Day begin.
'Tis then across the waters that the earliest sunlight laves
The myriad spirit forms that throng that pathway o'er the waves,
The beings that come to take the form and humble garb of man,

That come to labour and to love, to tread their destined
    span
Of sorrow, sickness, and despair, of evil years and few,
Before the Potter comes to make the broken vessels new.

We fathers, and our fathers saw, before ye White Men
    came,
Yon mighty Giant heave in sleep, and breathe the sul-
    phurous flame;
Have seen him roused to anger, lash these seas in furious
    wrath,
And all the torrents of his ire in lightning pouring forth;
Have seen him ever wrapt in smoke, and his tremendous
    form
For ever shrouded in his robe—his night robe of the
    storm;
But never saw his rugged sides bared to the day, till ye
Brake through the mighty Gates as gods, the Masters of
    the Sea.

Once from some nation far away two wand'ring hunters
    strayed,
Their birch canoe all patched and old, their dress of deer-
    skin made;
They rested in our Chieftain's lodge beside the stormy
    bay
Ere towards the setting sun in peace they should pursue
    their way.
They came towards the setting sun to seek his resting-
    place,
Where all the spirits of our dead and all the human race
Dwell where the sky is ever bath'd in floods of sunset
    light,—
The everlasting eventide that knows not death, or night,

Or fire or flood, or drought or war, where winter never
   reigns,
To the far happy Hunting Grounds upon the Golden
   Plains.

But when men of the Giant spoke, and his deep shroud
   of gloom,
And when they saw across the bay the clouded mountain
   loom,
And heard of the dread Thunder Bird whose nest is in the
   height,
Who guards the unassailed cliffs all wrapt in endless
   night;
And heard their fate who dared to seek his nest, and
   bring us down
The wondrous sacred medicine hid upon the mountain
   crown;—
They laughed our fears to scorn, and said, "Should
   brave men danger fear?
And what is danger, if it bring the Life Hereafter near?
He who hath sought through doubt and dread the
   Mystery of Life,
And won a blessing for Mankind by warring giant strife
With deathless gods, hath vanquish'd death, and in his
   body slain
Lust, wrath, and darkness, self, and shame; and from a
   beast's flesh free
Stands naked—man—"
      So, o'er the breast of that still
   moonlit sea
Led by the stranger braves we sped; and all the night
   time long
The startled clouds fled past the moon, the sad wind's
   dirge-like song

Wail'd in vague echoes down the heights, and moaned
    across the bay,
And moaned in tremulous low sighs from great cliffs far
    away.

So on the strangers sped :—the spray that from their
    paddles gleam'd
Made in the wake a path, whereon our long procession
    stream'd
A cortège to the grave; it seemed that in that midnight
    gloom
Huge enemies stalked by and frown'd, and moments big
    with doom
Fled wailing lost into the night. Oh, why should brave
    men die,
While coward hearts of thousands fail, and, wing'd with
    terror, fly !

So, when the East was cold with dawn, and all the clouds
    were grey,
The shadow of the mountain loom'd against the wak'ning
    day.
'Twas then an earnest conclave pray'd that Manitou
    should save
The strangers who amid the clouds sought wisdom or a
    grave.
The agates rattled as their skiff touch'd light the sombre
    main,—
We heard the solemn thunders warn, but warn the braves
    in vain.
With red plumes waving as they strode, they passed
    along the shore
To where a clouded canyon loom'd through broken rocks
    and hoar ;

And high the ancient cliffs soar'd up on every side around,
And at their base the fragments lay, and brushwood strew'd the ground.
They, clamb'ring o'er the boulders, leapt from rock to rock, and climb'd
Right up amid the canyon's gloom, till troubled sight and mind
Had lost the tiny spots that moved among the shadows vast,
And every vestige of their forms passed from our sight at last.

Then morning instant sank to gloom, and gloom was steep'd in night,
The waters all so late at rest had crests of foaming white;
Our prayers assail'd and storm'd the heaven for tender youth, and age,
And the Great Spirit saved our barks amid the cyclone's rage.
The hurricanes swept by—a lull—a blast—a loud wild cry—
From the rent altitudes, the towers, and battlements on high;
And ancient crags crash'd down the heights, and, lo, each breaking wave
Scream'd in his triumph round a crag, and bounded o'er its grave!
The Giant shook with wrath; the trees, uprooted, hurl'd in space;
A hail of monster spears were shot adown the mountain face;
Against the precipice on high the wildest breakers hurl'd,
And round a whirlpool's circling deeps the broken waters swirl'd;

And who can tell the lightning's glare, recount the
    thunder's roar,
Or the fierce shrieks that through the gloom the vengeful
    cyclones bore!

How long the tempests swept the bay, how long we
    fought for life,
How long among the lodges mourn'd the aged, child,
    and wife;
How long before we saw the smoke of camp-fires far
    away,
Just where the Kaministiquia is emptied in the bay;
How long we slept, and wearied lay, restored to home at
    last—
We could not tell, but heard the squaws relate four days
    were past
Since they had seen the tempest rage about the Giant's
    bed,
And saw the seas contend with heaven, and mourned their
    braves for dead.

Full many suns were set behind the darksome western
    height,
And still the tempest roar'd by day and lightning glared
    by night,
And still these dark cliffs answer'd loud the thunders
    from the bay;
The forests dared not sleep by night, the beasts were
    dumb by day!
We prayed that Manitou should aid the strangers to
    escape,—
'Twas then we named this "Thunder Bay," the moun-
    tain "Thunder Cape."

At last the shades of evening crept across the mighty sea,
When all the waters slept at last, the cloud-chained sky
    was free;
And all the great blue vault on high was echoed in the deep,
And floating in two azure skies the mountains lay asleep;
Then, as the waning sunlight flushed the crested cliffs on
    high,
There came to us a lone canoe across the nether sky.
It came not urged by sail or blade, but as a mother's
    breast
The bearing waters nestled it and laid it in its rest.
The little ripples at the sides laughed in their heedless
    play,
And in that cradle of the sea a dying warrior lay.

We laid him down beside the tents, and death-shades,
    like the night,
Upon his face were chased away by the red sunset light.
His dim eyes opened, and he spoke, but in the voice was
    told
The fever spirit dwelt within; in each stern feature's mould
We saw that youth was changed to age, since on the
    mountain side
We ceased to find him in the gloom, and hope grew sick
    and died.

"I see the thunder-clouds stoop down, and with their
    lean hands grasp
And hurl abroad their lightning fires—the mad winds
    halt and gasp—
The hills are sweating in their fear—the weary Air is
    slain—
The very crags crouch down and hide upon the upper
    plain.

The storm is breaking—lo, the trees as hail are hurl'd in
    space—
And all the huge rocks glow with fire along the mountain
    face;
From all the mountain mighty flames in fell contortion
    soar,
And through a whirling rain of fire unearthly cyclones
    roar!
In this great storm unaided man a thousand deaths had
    died—
Break Giant all this world to nought—Avenge—Thou art
    defied!
And thou, inviolate Thunder, hail, for Man has raped
    thy hold,
Thy nest is desecrate at last—the mighty secret told—
He strikes! And death is near—is come! Erect thy
    pride, my friend—
Lay down the life but not the man, for death is *not* the
    End!
And he is dead—and I shall live to tell to all mankind
The vulture Death is slain by death, and deathless reigns
    the Mind.
But oh the price!—For he is gone—he who had won the
    fight;
He who alone had grasped the Truth from that abyss of
    night—
By fire, by fever, or in fight, by lightning, ice, or wave,
There never sank a braver man than to yon hero's grave."

A mightier hero still than he who on the mountain died
Lay by the Kaministiquia.
                      Now all the bars aside,
And mighty barriers of death, were melted in the light
That stream'd from out the courts of Heaven o'er all the
    realms of Night.

The kingdom of the Life to Come reigned once o'er
    earthly sin,
For sunset opens wide the gates to let the dead come in;
The Land of the Hereafter lay before our straining eyes,
The amethystine glories flashed across the amber skies;
And in that light the Hero lay, and closed his eyes and
    slept—
The silver mists upon his brow their tears of parting
    wept—
So all the air was filled with light, and all the earth with
    rest
As that brave Spirit took the trail that leads towards the
    West.

IX.—SEASONS.

IX.—SEASONS.

HEAT.

Archibald Lampman.

From plains that seek to southward dim,
    The road runs by me white and bare;
Up the steep hill it seems to swim
    Beyond, and melt into the glare.
Upward, half-way, or it may be
    Nearer the summit, slowly steals
A haycart, moving duskily,
    With idly clacking wheels.

By his cart's side the waggoner
    Is slouching slowly at his ease,
Half-hidden in the windless blur
    Of white dust puffing to his knees.
This waggon on the height above,
    From sky to sky on either hand,
Is the sole thing that seems to move
    In all the heat-held land.

Beyond me, in the fields, the sun
   Soaks in the grass, and hath his will;
I count the marguerites one by one;
   Even the buttercups are still.
On the brook yonder not a breath
   Disturbs the spider or the midge;
The water-bugs draw close beneath
   The cool gloom of the bridge.

Where the far elm-tree shadows flood
   Dark patches in the burning grass,
The cows, each with her peaceful cud,
   Lie waiting for the heat to pass.
From somewhere on the slope near by,
   Into the pale depth of the noon
A wandering thrush slides leisurely
   His thin revolving tune.

In intervals of dreams I hear
   The cricket from the droughty ground;
The grasshoppers spin into mine ear
   A small immeasurable sound.
I lift mine eyes sometimes to gaze,
   The burning sky-line blinds my sight;
The woods far off are blue with haze,
   The hills are drenched in light.

And yet to me, not this or that
   Is always sharp or always sweet;
In the sloped shadow of my hat
   I lean at rest and drain the heat.
Nay more, I think some blessed power
   Hath brought me wandering idly here;
In the full furnace of this hour
   My thoughts grow keen and clear.

THE FIR WOODS.

Charles G. D. Roberts.

The wash of endless waves is in their tops,
   Endlessly swaying, and the long winds stream
   Athwart them from the far-off shores of dream.
Thro' the stirred branches filtering, faintly drops
Mystic dream-dust of isle, and palm, and cave,
   Coral and sapphire, realms of roses, that seem
   More radiant than ever earthly gleam
Revealed of fairy mead or haunted wave.

A cloud of gold, a cleft of blue profound,—
   These are my gates of wonder, surged about
     By tumult of tossed bough and rocking crest.
The vision lures; the spirit spurns her bound,
   Spreads her imprisoned wing, and drifts from out
     This green and humming gloom that wraps my rest.

CLOUDS.

Archibald Lampman.

The dew is gleaming in the grass,
   The morning hours are seven;
And I am fain to watch you pass,
   Ye soft white clouds of heaven.

Ye stray and gather, part and fold;
   The wind alone can tame you;
I dream of what in time of old
   The poets loved to name you.

They called you sheep, the sky your sward;
   A field, without a reaper;
They called the shining sun your lord,
   The shepherd wind your keeper.

Your sweetest poets I will deem
   The men of old for moulding,
In simple beauty, such a dream,—
   And I could lie beholding,

Where daisies in the meadow toss,
   The wind from morn till even
For ever shepherd you across
   The shining field of heaven.

FROGS.

Charles G. D. Roberts.

Here, in the red heart of the sunset lying,
   My rest an islet of brown weeds blown dry,
   I watch the wide bright heavens hovering nigh,
My plain and pools in lucent splendours dyeing!
My view dreams over the rosy wastes, descrying
   The reed-tops fret the solitary sky;
   And all the air is tremulous to the cry
Of myriad frogs on mellow pipes replying.

For the unrest of passion, here is peace;
   And eve's cool drench for midday soil and taint!
To tirèd ears, how sweetly brings release
   This limpid babble from life's unstilled complaint;
   While under tirèd eye-lids, lapse and faint
The noon's derisive visions,—fade and cease!

TWILIGHT.

Charles Heavysege.

The day was lingering in the pale north-west,
   And night was hanging o'er my head,—
   Night where a myriad stars were spread;
While down in the east, where the light was least,
   Seemed the home of the quiet dead.
   And, as I gazed on the field sublime,
   To watch the bright pulsating stars,
   Adown the deep, where the angels sleep,
   Came drawn the golden chime
   Of those great spheres that sound the years
   For the horologe of time;—
Millenniums numberless they told,
Millenniums a millionfold
   From the ancient hour of prime!

A CANADIAN SUMMER EVENING.

Mrs. Leprohon.

The rose-tints have faded from out of the west,
From the mountain's high peak, from the river's
   broad breast,
And silently shadowing valley and rill
The twilight steals noiselessly over the hill.
Behold, in the blue depths of ether afar,
Now softly emerging each glittering star;
While later the moon, placid, solemn, and bright,
Floods earth with her tremulous silvery light.

Hush! list to the whip-poor-will's soft plaintive notes,
As up from the valley the lonely sound floats;
Inhale the sweet breath of yon shadowy wood,
And the wild flowers blooming in hushed solitude.
Start not at the whispering, 'tis but the breeze,
Low rustling 'mid maple and lonely pine trees,
Or willows and alders that fringe the dark tide
Where canoes of the red men oft silently glide.

See, rising from out of that copse, dark and damp,
The fire-flies, each bearing a flickering lamp!
Like meteors, gleaming and streaming, they pass
O'er hillside and meadow, and dew-laden grass;
Contrasting with ripple on river and stream,
Alternately playing in shadow and beam,
Till fulness of beauty fills hearing and sight
Throughout the still hours of a calm summer night.

EVENING ON THE MARSHES.
Barry Straton.

We have roamed the marshes, keen with expectation,
    Lain at eve in ambush, where the ducks are wont to fly;
Felt the feverish fervour, the thrilling, full pulsation,
    As the flocks came whirring from the rosy western sky.

All day long the sun with heat, and breeze with coolness,
    Smote or kissed the grasses, and it seemed another lake
Flooded o'er the land and up the hills in fulness,—
    Shadows for the billows, sunshine for the waves that break.

Now beneath the pine, whose branches voice the breezes,
  Past the toil of day, we lie like gods in utter peace;
This is life's full nectar, this from care releases,—
  Oh, to rest for ever here where toil and tumult cease!

Slowly down the west the weary day is dying;
  Slowly up the east ascends the mellow, mystic moon;
Swiftly swoop the hawks; the hooting owls are flying;
  Through the darksome splendour breaks the lonesome cry of loon.

Ghost-like move the sails along the lake's dim distance;
  Faintly wafts the sailors' weirdsome song the waters o'er;
Faint the wavelets' music, as with low insistence,
  Break they softly singing on the drowsy sandy shore.

Wooing us in whispers, water, earth, and heaven,—
  Mystic whispers, wafted o'er the darksome waving deep,—
Win us to themselves, our old creative leaven,
  And we, mingling with them, softly sink to dreamless sleep.

MIDSUMMER NIGHT.

Archibald Lampman.

Mother of balms and soothings manifold,
  Quiet-breathèd Night, whose brooding hours are seven,
    To whom the voices of all rest are given,

And those few stars whose scattered names are told.
Far off, beyond the westward hills outrolled,
  Darker than thou, more still, more dreamy even,
  The golden moon leans in the dusky heaven.
And under her, one star, a point of gold.

And all go slowly lingering toward the west,
As we go down forgetfully to our rest,
  Weary of daytime, tired of noise and light.
Ah, it was time that thou shouldst come, for we
Were sore athirst, and had great need of thee,
  Thou sweet physician, balmy-bosomed Night.

OCTOBER.

Alexander M'Lachlan.

See how the great old forest vies
With all the glory of the skies,
  In streaks without a name;
And leagues on leagues of scarlet spires,
And temples lit with crimson fires,
  And palaces of flame!
And domes on domes that gleam afar,
Through many a gold and crimson bar,
  With azure overhead;
While forts, with towers on towers arise,
As if they meant to scale the skies,
  With banner bloody red!

Here, orange groves that seem asleep;
There, stately avenues that sweep
  To where the land declines;

There, starting up in proud array,
With helmets flashing to the day,
   Troop upon troop of pines!
Here, evergreens that have withdrawn,
And hang around the open lawn,
   With shadows creeping back;
While yonder, girdled hemlocks run
Like fiery serpents to the sun,
   Upon their gleaming track!

And, in the distance far apart,
As if to shame man's proudest art,
   Cathedral arches spread;
While yonder ancient elm has caught
A glory, 'yond the reach of thought,
   Upon his hoary head.
But every object, far and wide—
The very air is glorified—
   A perfect dream of bliss!
Earth's greatest painters never could,
Nor poet in inspirèd mood,
   Imagine aught like this.

O what are all ambition's gains!
What matters it who rules or reigns
   While I have standing here!
Gleams of unutterable things,
The work of the great King of kings!
   God of the full-crown'd year!
October! thou'rt a marvellous sight,
And with a rapture of delight
   We hail thy gorgeous pinion;
To elevate our hearts thou'rt here,
To bind us with a tie more dear
   To our beloved Dominion!

FIRST SNOW.

John Talon-Lespérance—"Laclède."

    The sun burns pale and low
Along the gloomy avenue of pines,
And the grey mist hangs heavily in lines
    Above the torrent's flow.

    I hear, on the violet hill,
The caw of blackbirds fleeing from the cold;
And buzz of insects, hiding in the mould,
    Under the ruined mill.

    The deep embrownèd wood
Is garlanded with wreaths of fleecy white;
And the stark poplar stands, a Northland sprite,
    Muffled in snowy hood.

    Afar, the cottage roof
Glistens with gems; the bridge that spans the drain
Is carpeted with down; the harvest plain
    Gleams 'neath a crystal woof.

    Heigh ho! The silver bells—
The gaudy sleighs that glide so merrily along—
The crunch of skipping hoofs—the woodman's song
    Loud echoing in the dells!

    The pine-knots cheerily blaze,
And shed a genial heat in wealthy homes;
The lords of earth, immured in cosy rooms,
    Heed not the wintry haze.

  But, in the dark damp lanes,
Where shrinks the pauper girl in filth and rags,
How dismally falls the snow upon the flags,
  Athwart the broken panes!

  With quick convulsive breath,
And hollow cough, the hopeless sufferers greet
In cruel winter's snow and ice and sleet
  The harbingers of death.

  Ay! But chief, on thy headstone,
Who slept 'neath summer roses, cold flakes rest,
And filter icy drops upon thy breast,—
  Thy tender breast—my own!

  While on my drooping head—
Yea, on my sunken heart—distils the snow,
Chilling the warmth and life that in its glow,
  In pity for my dead!

  Not till the crocus bloom,
And April rays have thawed the frost-bound slope,
O Rita, shall this heart to light re-ope,
  With the flowers on thy tomb!

INDIAN SUMMER.

William Wilfred Campbell.

Along the line of smoky hills
  The crimson forest stands,
And all the day the blue-jay calls
  Throughout the autumn lands.

Now by the brook the maple leans,
  With all his glory spread;
And all the sumachs on the hills
  Have turned their green to red.

Now, by great marshes wrapt in mist,
  Or past some river's mouth,
Throughout the long still autumn day
  Wild birds are flying south.

AN INDIAN SUMMER CAROL.
"Fidelis."

ALL day the dreamy sunshine steeps
  In gold the yellowing beeches,
In softest blue the river sleeps
  Among the island reaches.

Against the distant purple hills
  Rich autumn tints are glowing;
Its blood-red wine the sumach spills,
  Deep hues of carmine showing.

Upon the glassy stream the boat
  Glides softly, like a vision;
And, with its shadow, seems to float
  Among the isles Elysian.

About the plumy golden-rod
  The tireless bee is humming,
While crimson blossoms star the sod
  And wait the rover's coming.

The birch and maple glow with dyes
  Of scarlet, rose, and amber;
And, like a flame from sunset skies
  The tangled creepers clamber.

The oaks a royal purple wear,
  Gold-crowned where sunlight presses;
The birch stands like a Dryad fair
  Beneath her golden tresses.

So still the air—so like a dream—
  We hear the acorn falling;
And, o'er the scarcely rippled stream,
  The loon's long-quavered calling.

The robin softly, o'er the lea,
  A farewell song is trilling;
The squirrel flits from tree to tree
  Its winter storehouse filling.

Like him, we too may gather store
  From all this glorious Nature;
Then leave, my friend, your bookish lore
  And dreary nomenclature.

Leave the old thinkers to their dreams,
  The treasures of the ages;
Leave dusty scientific reams,
  And study Nature's pages.

Her poetry is better far
  Than all men write about her;
Old Homer's song of love and war
  Had scarce been sung without her.

Haste to the wood,—put books away,
  They'll wait the tardy comer;
For *them* there's many a winter day,
  But brief's our Indian summer!

A MID-WINTER NIGHT'S DREAM.

William Wilfred Campbell.

The snows outside are white and white;
The gusty flue shouts through the night;
And by the lonely chimney light
  I sit and dream of Summer.

The orchard bough creaks in the blast,
That like a ghost goes shrieking past,
And coals are dying fast and fast,
  But still I dream of Summer.

'Tis not the voice of falling rain,
Or dream wind blown through latticed pane,
When earth will laugh in green again,
  That makes me dream of Summer.

But hopes will then have backward flown,
Like fleets of promise, long outblown,
And Love once more will greet his own;
  This is my dream of Summer.

WINTER NIGHT.

Charles Heavysege.

The stars are setting in the frosty sky,
   Numerous as pebbles on a broad sea-coast;
While o'er the vault the cloud-like galaxy
   Has marshalled its innumerable host.
Alive all heaven seems; with wondrous glow,
   Tenfold refulgent every star appears;
As if some wide, celestial gale did blow,
   And thrice illume the ever-kindled spheres.

Orbs, with glad orbs rejoicing, burning, beam,
   Ray-crowned, with lambent lustre in their zones;
Till o'er the blue, bespangled spans seem
   Angels and great archangels on their thrones;
A host divine, whose eyes are sparkling gems,
And forms more bright than diamond diadems.

ICICLE DROPS.

Arthur John Lockhart.

I.

Fast from yon icicle's inverted spire,
   Yon shining minims, glittering in the sun,
Fall brightly down, sheen drops of fluent fire,
   Momently hanging,—sinking, one by one,—
Sliding clear beads as down a silver wire;
   So archer-stars shoot thro' abysses dun;
So blood drips down from the knive's fierce desire;
   So fall our moments; so our tears do run.

With drop on drop, with everlasting flow,
  With changing atom, and revolving sphere,
Our never-resting lives must downward go;—
  Still hung in momentary brightness here,
Then sinking to that breast toward which incline
The drops that glow, and eke the beams that shine.

II.

The sun, at length, with a more fervent fire,
  Hath gained a subtle mastery of the dawn;
And, still more swiftly, from the less'ning spire
  The hastening gems descend, till all are gone.
But, lo! they come! The vanish'd ones surprise
  In golden mist, my wistful, musing sight;
Soul o' th' earth, its exhalations rise,
  And soon the drops return to air and light.

There shall they hang 'mid purple glooms aloof,
  With clouds noon-white, or tinct with crimson eve;
Or shine supreme in Iris' circling woof,
  Wherein his married hues the sun doth weave.
And so this falling life shall not remain
Sunk in the earth; 'twill rise to Heaven again.

THE SILVER FROST.

Barry Straton.

A breath from the tropics broke Winter's spell
With an alien rain which froze as it fell,
And ere the Orient blushed with morn
A beautiful crystal forest was born.

Blackthorn hedge and hawthorn bush
Dawned spectrally white in the first grey flush:
Drifted from night the circling trees
As icebergs drift from northern seas.

Branch above branch, an aerial maze
Of pendulous crystals and silvery sprays!
Tree behind tree impregnable,
Where beauty, and silence, and sweet thoughts dwell!

The elm boughs bend, like a searching thought,
With their silvery weight of beauty caught.
White limbs are asleep on the misty blue skies
Like lilies on lakelets in paradise.

Daylight refulgent floods over the hills,
And the forest, conscious of beauty, thrills.
Through the mazes of fragile mimicry
The dazzling sunrays flare and flee.

Pine, elm, and maple, in icy attire,
Burn with a myriad gems of fire.
The snow-billowed ground and the gossamer height
Are aflame with the scornful spirit of light.

Violet, orange, indigo, red,
Green, yellow, and blue from each diamond are shed:
More beautiful these than the jewels of a throne,
For the forest is nature's glory and crown.

The grape-vine over the lilacs laid
Gleams like a rainbowed, tossed cascade,
And he who beholds might pause to hear
The enlivened voices of waters there.

In the Balm of Gilead and poplar's spire
Are incarnate the spirits of water and fire:
In cedar and linden, and everywhere,
The flames of the passionless fires flare.

But wandering winds the frail boughs shake
And rustling ripples of ruin awake,
And a myriad scintillant gems fall down,
Like thoughts transfigured of beauties flown.

THE JEWELLED TREES.

George Martin.

I.

On the verge of the month of the white new year,
When friend to friend gives heartiest cheer,
The rain and the frost for a night and a day
Have cunningly worked alternately.
They have thickened the crust of the dazzling snow
Over whose surface the cold winds blow;
They have fringed the eaves with their old device,
Enormous daggers of glittering ice;
And the nails in the walls, where in summer time
The scarlet-runners were wont to climb,
They have crowned with gems more bright, more fair,
Than eastern queens on their bosoms wear.
But scarcely a glance do we waste on these,
For our wonder is fixed on the jewelled trees;
Never before, in all their days,
Have they borne such beauty for mortal gaze;
On them the frost and the rain have wrought
A splendour that could not be sold or bought,

Heavily laden from foot to crown,
Like fairest of brides with heads bowed down,
In park and square, demurely they stand,—
Stand by the wayside all over the land.
Thick-crusted with pearls of marvellous size,
Whose lustre rebukes our aching eyes.

II.

Thus for a night and a day have they stood,
Modest and chaste in their virginhood;
But are they as happy, as joyful at heart,
As when, in green vesture, they gladly took part
In all the fresh bliss that to spring-time they owed,—
In all the hot pleasure that summer bestowed?
" Nay, verily, nay!" I hear them repeat;
The blood in our veins, even down to our feet,
Is gelid and still,—we are sick unto death;
Oh send us, ye heavens! oh send us a breath
Of warmth that will bear all these jewels away!
These fetters that we for a night and day
Have borne in silence with infinite pain.
Oh give us our freedom! our bare arms again!"

III.

A wind that had slept all this time in the south,
In an orange grove that was faint from drouth,
Heard the soft plaint of the jewelled trees,
And came in the guise of a gentle breeze,—
Came, and with kisses tenderly
Unbound the captives, and set them free.
Their crystalline chains were broken asunder,
Filling all earth with a blinding wonder;—
With a crash and a flash and a musical sound,
Like a shower of stars they fell to the ground;

And, freed from their bondage, the grateful trees
In their bare brown arms caressed the breeze,
Caressed the wind that came from the south,
From the orange grove that was faint from drouth;
And they wept for joy, their thanks they wept,
While the wind lay still in their arms and slept.

IN LYRIC SEASON.

Bliss Carman.

The lyric April time is forth
  With lyric mornings, frost and sun;
  From leaguers vast of night undone
Auroral mild new stars are born.

And ever at the year's return,
  Along the valleys grey with rime,
  Thou leadest as of old, where time
Can nought but follow to thy sway.

The trail is far through leagues of Spring
  And long the quest to the white core
  Of harvest quiet, yet once more
I gird me to the old unrest.

I know I shall not ever meet
  Thy calm regard across the year,
  And yet I know thou wilt draw near,
Nor stir the hour asleep on guard.

    Beside the orchard, when athwart
      The dusk, a meteor's gleam unbars
      God's lyric of the April stars
    Above the autumn hills of dream.

THE FROGS.*

Archibald Lampman.

Breathers of wisdom won without a quest,
    Quaint, uncouth dreamers, voices high and strange,
    Flutist of lands, where beauty hath no change,
And wintery grief is a forgotten guest;
Sweet murmurers of everlasting rest,
    For whom glad days have ever yet to run,
    And moments are as æons, and the sun
But ever half-way sunken toward the west.

Often to me who heard you in your day,
    With close-wrapped ears, it could not choose but seem
That earth, our mother, searching in what way
    Men's hearts might know her spirit's inmost dream,
Ever at rest beneath life's change and stir,
Made you her soul, and bade you pipe for her.

In those mute days, when spring was in her glee,
    And hope was strong, we know not why or how,
    And earth, the mother, dreamed with brooding brow,

---

* The orchestras of frogs are a notable feature of settlement life. Their singing, in the distances of forest rivers, is really very musical.

Musing on life, and what the hours might be
   When love should ripen to maternity,
Then, like high flutes in silvery interchange,
Ye piped with voices still and sweet and strange,
   And ever as ye piped, on every tree

The great buds swelled; among the pensive woods
   The spirits of first flowers awoke, and flung
From buried faces the close-fitting hoods,
   And listened to your piping till they fell;
   The frail spring beauty, with her perfumed bell,
The wind flower, and the spotted adder tongue.

All the day long, wherever pools might be,
   Among the golden meadows, where the air
   Stood in a dream, as it were moorèd there
For ever in a noontide reverie;
Or where the birds made riot of their glee
   In the still woods, and the hot sun shone down,
   Crossed with warm shadows, on the brown
Leaf-paven pools, that bubbled dreamily;

Or far away in whispering river meads
   And watery marshes, where the brooding noon,
   Full with the wonder of its own sweet boon,
Nestled and slept among the noiseless reeds,
   Ye sat and murmured motionless as they
   With eyes that dreamed beyond the night and day.

And when day passed, and over heaven's height,
   Thin with the many stars, and cool with dew,
   The fingers of the deep hours slowly drew
The wonder of the ever-heating night,

No grief or loneliness, or wrapped delight,
  Or weight of silence, ever brought to you
  Slumber or rest; only your voices grew
More high and solemn.   Slowly with hushed flight

Ye saw the echoing hours go by, long drawn,
  Nor ever stirred, watching with fathomless eyes,
  And with your countless clear antiphonies
Filling the earth and heaven, even till dawn,
  Hast risen, found you with its first pale gleam,
  Still with soft throats unaltered in your dream.

And slowly, as we heard you day by day,
  The stillness of enchanted reveries
  Bound brain and spirit and half-closed eyes
In some divine sweet wonder dream astray;
To us no sorrow or upreared dismay,
  Nor any discord came; but ever more,
  The voices of mankind, the outer roar,
Grew strange and murmurous, faint and far away;

Morning and noon and midnight exquisitely,
  Wrapped with your voices, this alone we knew,
Cities might change and fall, and men might die,
  Secure were we, content to dream with you,
That change and pain are shadows faint and fleet,
And dreams are real, and life is only sweet.

THE CANADIAN SONG-SPARROW.
J. D. Edgar.

From the leafy maple ridges,
From the thickets of the cedar,
From the alders by the river,

From the bending willow branches,
From the hollows and the hillsides,
Through the lone Canadian forest,
Comes the melancholy music,
Oft repeated,—never changing,—
    "All—is—vanity—vanity—vanity."

Where the farmer ploughs his furrow,
Sowing seed with hope of harvest,
In the orchard white with blossom,
In the early field of clover,
Comes the little brown-clad singer,
Flitting in and out of bushes,
Hiding well behind the fences,
Piping forth his song of sadness,—
    "Poor—hu—manity—manity—manity."

IN JUNE.

The Canadian Rossignol on Mount Royal.

E. W. THOMSON.

PRONE where maples widely spread
I watch the far blue overhead,
Where little fine-spun clouds arise
From naught to naught before my eyes;
Within the shade a pleasant rout
Of dallying zephyrs steal about;
Lazily as moves the day
Odours float and faint away
From roses yellow, red, and white,
That prank yon garden with delight;

Round which the locust blossoms swing,
And some late lilacs droop for spring.
Anon swells up a dubious breeze
Stirring the half reluctant trees,
Then, rising to a mimic gale,
Ruffles the massy oak to pale
Till, spent its sudden force, once more
The zephyrs come that went before ;
Now silvery poplars shivering stand,
And languid lindens waver bland,
Hemlock traceries scarcely stir,
All the pines of summer purr.
Hovering butterflies I see,
Full of business shoots the bee,
Straight to yon valley is his flight
Where solemn marbles crowd so white.
Half hid in the grasses there
Red-breast thrushes jump and stare,
Sparrows flutter up like leaves
Tossed upon the wind in sheaves.
Curve-winged swallows slant and slide
O'er the graves that stretch so wide,
Steady crows go labouring by—
Ha ! the Rossignol is nigh !

Rossignol, why will you sing
Though lost the lovely world of spring?
'Twas well that then your roulades rang
Of joy, despite of every pang,
But now the sweet, the bliss is gone—
  Nay, now the summer joy is on,
  And lo, the foliage and the bloom,
  The fuller life the bluer room,
  'Twas this the sweet spring promised me.
O bird, and can you sing so free ?

And will you sing when summer goes
And leaves turn brown and dies the rose?
Oh, then how brave shall autumn dress
The maple out with gorgeousness!
And red-cheeked apples deck the green,
And corn wave tall its yellow sheen.
But, bird, bethink you well, I pray,
Then marches winter on his way.
Ah, winter—yes, ah, yes—but still,
Hark! sweetly chimes the summer rill,
And joy is here and life is strong,
And love still calls upon my song.
No, Rossignol, sing not that strain,
Triumphant 'spite of all the pain,—
She cannot hear you, Rossignol,
She does not pause and flush, your thrall.
She does not raise that slender hand
And, poised, lips parted, understand
What you are telling of the years
Her brown eyes soft with happy tears,
She does not hear a note of all.
Ah, Rossignol, ah, Rossignol!
But skies are blue, and flowers bloom,
And roses breathe the old perfume,
And here the murmuring of the trees
In all of lovelier mysteries—
And maybe now she hears my song
Pouring the summer hills along,
Listens with joy that still to thee
Remain the summer time and me.

THE WALTER SCOTT PRESS, NEWCASTLE-ON-TYNE.

THE CANTERBURY POETS.

EDITED BY WILLIAM SHARP.

IN SHILLING VOLUMES, CLOTH, SQUARE 8VO.

Cloth, Red Edges	. 1s.	Red Roan, Gilt Edges, 2s. 6d
Cloth, Uncut Edges .	. 1s.	Pad. Morocco, Gilt Edges - 5s.

Christian Year.	Early English Poetry.
Coleridge.	Sea Music.
Longfellow.	Herrick.
Campbell.	Ballades and Rondeaus.
Shelley.	Irish Minstrelsy.
Wordsworth.	Milton's Paradise Lost.
Blake.	Jacobite Ballads.
Whittier.	Australian Ballads.
Poe.	Moore's Poems.
Chatterton.	Border Ballads.
Burns. Poems.	Song-Tide.
Burns. Songs.	Odes of Horace.
Marlowe.	Ossian.
Keats.	Elfin Music.
Herbert.	Southey.
Victor Hugo.	Chaucer.
Cowper.	Poems of Wild Life.
Shakespeare:	Paradise Regained.
Songs, Poems, and Sonnets.	Crabbe.
Emerson.	Dora Greenwell.
Sonnets of this Century.	Goethe's Faust.
Whitman.	American Sonnets.
Scott. Marmion, etc.	Landor's Poems.
Scott. Lady of the Lake, etc.	Greek Anthology.
Praed.	Hunt and Hood.
Hogg.	Humorous Poems.
Goldsmith.	Lytton's Plays.
Mackay's Love Letters.	Great Odes.
Spenser.	Owen Meredith's Poems.
Children of the Poets.	Painter-Poets.
Ben Jonson.	Women-Poets.
Byron (2 Vols.).	Love Lyrics.
Sonnets of Europe.	American Humor. Verse.
Allan Ramsay.	Scottish Minor Poets.
Sydney Dobell.	Cavalier Lyrists.
Days of the Year.	German Ballads.
Pope.	Songs of Beranger.
Heine.	Poems by Roden Noel.
Beaumont and Fletcher.	Songs of Freedom.
Bowles, Lamb, etc.	Canadian Poems.

London: WALTER SCOTT, LIMITED, 24 Warwick Lane.

LIBRARY OF HUMOUR.

Cloth Elegant, Large Crown 8vo.   Price 3/6 per volume.

VOLUMES ALREADY ISSUED.

THE HUMOUR OF FRANCE. Translated, with an Introduction and Notes, by Elizabeth Lee. With numerous Illustrations by Paul Frénzeny.

THE HUMOUR OF GERMANY. Translated, with an Introduction and Notes, by Hans Müller-Casenov. With numerous Illustrations by C. E. Brock.

THE HUMOUR OF ITALY. Translated, with an Introduction and Notes, by A. Werner. With 50 Illustrations by Arturo Faldi.

THE HUMOUR OF AMERICA. Edited, with an Introduction and Notes, by J. Barr (of the *Detroit Free Press*). With numerous Illustrations by C. E. Brock.

VOLUMES IN PREPARATION.

THE HUMOUR OF HOLLAND. Translated, with an Introduction and Notes, by A. Werner. With numerous Illustrations by Dudley Hardy.

THE HUMOUR OF IRELAND. Selected by D. J. O'Donoghue. With numerous Illustrations by Oliver Paque.

THE HUMOUR OF RUSSIA. Translated, with Notes, by E. L. Boole, and an Introduction by Stepniak. With 50 Illustrations by Paul Frénzeny.

THE HUMOUR OF SPAIN. Translated, with an Introduction and Notes, by S. Taylor. With numerous Illustrations by H. R. Millar.

To be followed by volumes representative of ENGLAND, SCOTLAND, JAPAN, etc. The Series will be complete in about twelve volumes.

London: WALTER SCOTT, LIMITED, 24 Warwick Lane.

COMPACT AND PRACTICAL.

In Limp Cloth; for the Pocket. Price One Shilling.

THE EUROPEAN
CONVERSATION BOOKS.

FRENCH. **ITALIAN.**
SPANISH. **GERMAN.**
NORWEGIAN.

CONTENTS.

Hints to Travellers—Everyday Expressions—Arriving at and Leaving a Railway Station—Custom House Enquiries—In a Train—At a Buffet and Restaurant—At an Hotel—Paying an Hotel Bill—Enquiries in a Town—On Board Ship—Embarking and Disembarking—Excursion by Carriage—Enquiries as to Diligences—Enquiries as to Boats—Engaging Apartments—Washing List and Days of Week—Restaurant Vocabulary—Telegrams and Letters, etc., etc.

The contents of these little handbooks are so arranged as to permit direct and immediate reference. All dialogues or enquiries not considered absolutely essential have been purposely excluded, nothing being introduced which might confuse the traveller rather than assist him. A few hints are given in the introduction which will be found valuable to those unaccustomed to foreign travel.

London: WALTER SCOTT, LIMITED, 24 Warwick Lane.

NEW EDITION IN NEW BINDING.

In the new edition there are added about forty reproductions in fac-simile of autographs of distinguished singers and instrumentalists, including Sarasate, Joachim, Sir Charles Hallé, Paderewsky, Stavenhagen, Henschel, Trebelli, Miss Macintyre, Jean Gérardy, etc.

Quarto, cloth elegant, gilt edges, emblematic design on cover, 6s. May also be had in a variety of Fancy Bindings.

THE
MUSIC OF THE POETS:
A MUSICIANS' BIRTHDAY BOOK.

EDITED BY ELEONORE D'ESTERRE KEELING.

THIS is a unique Birthday Book. Against each date are given the names of musicians whose birthday it is, together with a verse-quotation appropriate to the character of their different compositions or performances. A special feature of the book consists in the reproduction in fac-simile of autographs, and autographic music, of living composers. Three sonnets by Mr. Theodore Watts, on the "Fausts" of Berlioz, Schumann, and Gounod, have been written specially for this volume. It is illustrated with designs of various musical instruments, etc.; autographs of Rubenstein, Dvorâk, Greig, Mackenzie, Villiers Stanford, etc., etc.

London: WALTER SCOTT, LTD., 24 Warwick Lane

www.ingramcontent.com/pod-product-compliance
Lightning Source LLC
Chambersburg PA
CBHW031905220426
43663CB00006B/774